Limitless Mind

Complete Step by Step Guide on How to Develop a
Limitless Mind to Increase Your Potential and
Broaden Your Capacity

Improve Yourself Series - Book 7

GARRETT REDFIELD

TABLE OF CONTENTS

CONTENTS

INTRODUCTION

Have you ever been told that your potential is limited? That you're a failure? Dumb? Incapable? It is all too easy to listen to these negative thoughts from others, and even adopt them and begin telling ourselves the same words that have caused us pain throughout our lives. After all, why should we believe in ourselves when nobody else does?

I'm here to bring you hope. You are capable of more. You can learn whatever you set your mind to. Your potential is limitless. You possess what you require to achieve more because you possess all that you need: a limitless mind.

Over the past several decades, scientists have been learning more about what the mind is capable of achieving and how. This culmination of knowledge allows us to actively improve our mind, shedding our chains, and soaring toward new heights. By putting together and acting on this scientific knowledge, your mind will gain the ability to learn, adapt, and develop like never before. Whether you are a student looking to do better in class, and adult wanting to learn a new skill or excel at work, or a teacher hoping to bestow the next generation with all the tools they need for limitless success, you can gain the knowledge you need to act on in the pages of this book.

There is no reason to allow yourself to remain chained by harsh words, fear, or insecurities. You can excel.

CHAPTER 1: LIMITLESS POTENTIAL WITH NEUROPLASTICITY

Have you ever felt as if your potential is locked-in and set in place? For many people, it feels as if their potential is a large stone wall that can't be broken through, preventing them from moving beyond the wall and attaining something more. What if I were to tell you that this wall is not actually the end of your potential, which you can't go past. Instead, this wall is made up of our preconceived notions and ideas that are holding us back. Yet, you don't have to allow this wall to hold you back. By learning your limitless potential, you can soar past the wall and go as far as you desire. You can learn more. You can work to attain your dreams. You can achieve whatever you put your mind to.

There are many reasons people develop the belief that their potential is limited. One common reason is due to outside influences. If a child does poorly learning in the standard classroom environment, then people can label them as a "failure," "difficult," "problem child," or "dumb." These words sting and stick with a person, especially children who are still growing and developing, and therefore more vulnerable to outside influences. Every year countless children feel like failures because they don't do well in school. And, as these children grow up, the negative feelings don't go away.

Often times, as such children grow up, they come to believe that there is a set limit to their potential that they can not surpass. Because of this, their grades never go up, they get overwhelmed with trying, and they give up. When looking to get into a college, they might believe their dream college is impossible, and that they will have to settle. They may even give up going to college altogether.

When it comes to entering the corporate world at the start of their careers, these feelings don't miraculously disappear. Rather, they continue to be held back by the chains of self-doubt. These beliefs of themselves that have been built up since childhood can prevent a person from excelling at work and getting promoted. Depending on how severe a person's self-doubt is, they might even do so poorly at their job that they are let go or fired.

Children and adults who are held back by chains of self-doubt and a wall of preconceived potential may have dreams for the future, but they remain as dreams. These people struggle to accept themselves and recognize their own abilities. These ideas prevent them from acting on and achieving their dreams to make them into a reality. But, it doesn't have to be this way.

Whether an adult or child, you can burst through your chains and soar over the wall to new heights and new potential. While this may seem far-fetched to someone who is plagued by self-doubt, it is long tried and true, and scientifically proven.

Plasticity - noun
Plas·tic·i·ty | pla-ˈsti-sə-tē
1: the quality or state of being plastic.
Especially: capacity for being molded or altered.
2: the ability to retain a shape attained by pressure deformation.
3: the capacity for continuous alteration of the neural pathways and synapses of the living brain and nervous system in response to experience or injury.

Science has proven time and again that the brain is astoundingly plastic. This means that our brains are continuously working, adapting, and reshaping based on our environments and actions. The walls and chains can't hold us back unless we allow them to. If we choose to fight against them, against the preconceived limitations and push forward, we can rewire our brains and reach new heights.

Does this sound impossible? To someone who is bound by their own thoughts and the harsh criticisms of others, it likely does. But, think about all humans have been able to attain throughout history. At times, what we now accept as a given reality was considered inconceivable. Few people thought humankind would actually walk on the moon, fly through the air, or have the ability to make a phone call to the other side of the planet. These ideas seemed impossible, absurd even. The inventors and pioneers of science who developed these technologies were ridiculed and mocked by many. Yet, they didn't allow the criticisms to hold them back and become chains to tie them down. They kept working, and through their tenacity and unwillingness to give in, they were able to soar past what was once thought possible.

This ability to attain more through effort and force of will is not only reserved for pioneers in science. These famous men and women weren't even always believed to be great geniuses. Many of them were mocked in their time, and it was only after they proved themselves that the perception of them changed. Each and every person can find this ability within themselves to surpass what they once thought was possible and succeed. You don't have to be a genius, have a high IQ, or come from a well-renowned family. Whether your dream is to increase your grades, get into your dream college, or get a promotion at work, with effort, knowledge, and neuroplasticity, you can attain what you once thought you were incapable of.

No matter a person's age, the brain is amazingly plastic. Often, this ability is thought to be reserved for young children as they age, learn, and adjust to the world around them. But it doesn't go away. Professor and Director of Harvard University's Mind, Brain, and Education Program, Kurt Fischer, is an expert on this. He explains that "the brain is remarkably plastic," and "even in the middle of old age, it's still adapting very actively to its environment." This means that even if you are twenty, thirty, fifty, or eighty, you can still utilize your neuroplasticity to learn, advance, and excel.

The phrase "you can't teach an old dog new tricks" is a popular one. It often makes people feel that they are too old to start something new. Yet, despite this phrase being used for centuries, it is not accurate. Not only can old dogs still be trained, people, no matter their age, can learn, grow, and develop. Scientists who frequently found this idiom to be false studied the concept and in the '90s began to better understand neuroplasticity. Now, with several decades of research completed, the scientific world has a much better understanding of how neuroplasticity works. A person can use this knowledge to teach themselves something new, whether they are a child or a senior adult.

While the brain still has many mysteries that scientists seek to answer, the understanding they have gained regarding neuroplasticity is one of the most fundamental and reliable understandings we have to date. They have proven and come to understand how our intelligence and potential aren't fixed from birth, genetics, or any other factors. Intelligence and potential are not static or fixed. Rather, we can continuously learn, grow, and change throughout the course of our lives. With a little understanding, you can directly harness your neuroplasticity to grow toward your goals. During the chapters of this book, you will learn how.

The brain is made up of gray matter and white matter. While the white matter is full of dendrites and axons that facilitate communication, the gray matter is full of billions of neurons that do the actual communication. This biological network may not be made up of muscle, but it behaves similarly in some ways. Mainly in the aspect of muscle memory. This form of learning requires doing an action countless times with your muscles, such as swinging a bat. A person may be a poor baseball player when they first begin swinging a bat, but after countless swings and hours of practice, the muscles will adapt and learn on their own. After practice, the muscles will automatically know how to swing the bat correctly, even without thought put into the action. This is how a baseball player can accurately hit a fastball that is coming at them too quickly for them to manually analyze and think about how to hit it. The muscles simply know what to do after countless hours of practice.

In the same way that muscles are able to develop and learn through consistent practice, so too can the neurons in the brain. Whenever you repeatedly access a memory or practice an activity, your neurons will repeatedly fire together in the same way, creating new pathways in your neural network. Your neural network will build itself around how you use it. So, if you regularly use your brain for mathematical equations, then the neural pathways for math will be more reactive and responsive. On the other hand, if you rarely practice math, you will likely find yourself struggling more to answer even basic equations. This is why many people are able to quickly and accurately use math that they require on a daily basis—such as $2+2$—but struggle when they get to less commonly used equations.

In the late '90s, scientists even created a slogan for this, which goes "cells that fire together, wire together." What this slogan means is that not only do repeatedly practiced tasks become quicker and easier for the brain to respond to overtime, but it acts as a domino effect. This domino effect means that if you fire one neuron in the sequence, the next neuron and the one after that are likely to follow. This means; eventually, you will have to think less about a task that has become ingrained in you. But, even if you are struggling to remember how to do a task, such as giving the right answer to an exam, if you are able to remember even a part of the answer, the rest of the answer will likely follow and come to you.

This aspect of neuroplasticity is the principle that the learning method known as the mnemonic device relies on. With the mnemonic device, you use an easily-remembered phrase to help knock down the dominoes in your neural network so that you can then remember more difficult information. For instance, you could use the phrase "Eat An Apple As A Nice Snack" to help you remember the seven continents. This works, as the first letter of each word correlates to the first letter of a continent, specifically "Europe, Asia, Africa, Australia, Antarctica, North America, and South America."

It's easy to fall into the habit of thinking that our brains the way they are at this moment is how they will always be. This is especially true in today's day in age, with technology and computers all around us. Nearly everyone is aware that when you purchase a computer, you might be able to update the software, but the hardware won't replace itself. Sure, you can take a computer apart and replace old hardware, but this is much more similar to a medical transplant rather than an update. Simply put, no matter how much you play or work on your computer, no matter how many keys or buttons you push, the hardware won't miraculously change itself. Everyone knows this. It is a basic principle you learn without realizing it when you first begin using a computer. Because of this, you might think that your brain works in a similar way; after all, the brain is often referred to as "the ultimate computer." Yet, the brain is amazing at adapting, much more so than an actual computer.

From prior to our birth and to the point of our death, our brains are constantly interacting with the environment around us and adapting based on its needs. The connections between our neurons realize what we are missing and will then act in response to create what we need. Not only are new pathways created, but old pathways that you no longer use and have fallen dormant over time will be recycled to create way for the new pathways. In this way, your brain is constantly restructuring itself so that you can learn, grow, and succeed, no matter the changes you go through in life. This process happens naturally on a daily basis, but it isn't something that you have no control over. You can harness this ability, stimulating and encouraging it so that you can better achieve your goals, no matter what they may be.

Now, while children and adults alike can benefit from and make use of neuroplasticity, this is not to say that there is no difference in the neuroplasticity of adults and children. But, by understanding this difference, you can make use of your brain's plastic ability to reach new heights, no matter your age.

First, let's look at the neuroplasticity of children and young adults. Children are always going through new experiences, growing, and developing. Because of this, their neurons have to be able to keep up with an incredibly rapid pace. When a child is born, their brain has approximately 7,500 neural connections; by the time they reach two-years-old, their neural connections have increased so much that they have more than double the number of the average adult. As the child ages, they will begin forming their own patterns in life, which will lead to new connections. But, while these new connections are being built, the old connections that they started out life with are no longer used or needed. Therefore, the brain prunes away the old connections that are no longer needed, so that the newer connections can be built larger and more sturdy, to support more difficult tasks.

While adults have fewer neural connections, this does not mean that they are less able to learn, adapt, and excel. The adult brain does not only have the ability to create new strong neural pathways but also to resurrect long lost connections that have been unused for quite some time. This is why if an adult hasn't used a skill for some time, such as painting, they may need a little time to warm up and adjust. But, before long, they will be back at their previous skill level, as the old pathway that was out of use has been revitalized. This level of neuroplasticity is even able to greatly enhance cognitive skills and memory. These abilities are boosted when an adult actively sustains a healthy lifestyle and utilizes skills aimed at harnessing neuroplasticity.

Neuroplasticity is all about learning. Therefore, whenever we learn, we should work to implement neuroplasticity and understand its nature. Every single time we begin to learn, whether in a classroom or not, the process of neuroplasticity actively works to create new pathways in the brain. This means that with every time we learn, we have the opportunity to completely change the way our brain automatically operates. It is truly an amazing and powerful gift.

However, while this is an amazing gift, it's not to say all learning is created equal. If that were the case, there would be no need for most people to learn about neuroplasticity. We would already be able to get the utmost out of it without even trying. But, the truth is, if we don't understand how to best use this remarkable system, we can allow a portion of our brain's plastic potential go to waste without ever making use of it to its full effect.

If you simply learn to memorize a list of facts, you likely won't be making use of the brain's neuroplasticity. On the other hand, learning to play an instrument, dance, or a new language will create those new pathways, thanks to neuroplasticity. You are, in effect, rewiring your brain through this type of learning.

To truly harness your neuroplasticity, you shouldn't only focus on it when you are actively trying to learn something new, but throughout your regular day-to-day life, as well. This is because studies have found that many of our lifestyle factors affect the plasticity of our neural pathways. To put it simply, if you live a poor lifestyle, even if you put a lot of effort into learning, you will simply be unable to get the most out of your neural pathways. Parents have long known that poor sleep, unhealthy diets, and a lack of physical activity can affect the minds and learning ability of their children, and they were right! Studies have now proven this to be true through neuroplasticity. Thankfully, this means we also know concrete and straight-forward ways you can improve your neuroplasticity.

One great way is to give a person an enriched

environment. This means an environment that poses challenges, novelty, and allow for stretches of focused attention. The best way to do this is to provide people with exciting things to learn in their daily life. It is important that they are truly excited about it. Otherwise, it won't be novel, and their focus will wane. Simply making a child sit and play the violin all day won't hone in on this benefit. But, by allowing children to excitedly learn about their passions, you can. Studies found that when children and young adults are provided such an environment, they are able to experience benefits of neuroplasticity into adulthood.

Practicing physical fitness and physical activities can increase the volume of the hippocampus, which allows for more neural pathways. It can even slow or altogether prevent the normal neural death and hippocampus damage caused by age. Simply put, it can slow or prevent reductions in neuroplasticity, keeping your brain malleable and allowing it to continue building new pathways, learning new things, and reaching new heights. It doesn't matter if your physical activity is a workout or an outdoor sport, challenging or gentle, as long as you keep your body active, it will boost the mind's potential.

Studies have found that sleep impairment, especially chronic sleep insufficiency, causes neuron death and damage, which is a breakdown of the brain's neural pathways and neuroplasticity. This means forgoing sleep when you have an important exam or deadline coming up does nothing but hinder any progress you want to make. On the other hand, by achieving adequate sleep, you can enhance your neurogenesis, and in the process, your neuroplasticity. This means if you are ever working on learning or achieving something, you should always prioritize high-quality regular sleep.

While children shouldn't practice intermittent fasting, as it will interfere with their health and growth, moderate intermittent fasting has been shown to promote neuron pathway response, allowing you to create new pathways more quickly. However, this is only effective if you practice intermittent fasting healthfully, without depriving yourself of needed calories. After all, it isn't just the muscles that require calories to function, but the brain, as well.

CHAPTER 2: EMBRACE MISTAKES FOR GREATER SUCCESS

For many people, mistakes are seen as a devastating outcome. For children and young adults especially, who are newly adjusting to dealing with mistakes and failure, these experiences can become an overwhelming burden. A child who struggles to read may want to give up on learning all-together. A teenager forced to learn the violin may become so overburdened with mistakes that they begin to hate music. When children experience these types of events in their formative years, they grow up to be adults struggling with perfectionism. Sure, it is good to try your best and accomplish your goals. But, there are many aspects of perfectionism that are detrimental. Often times, these perfectionists refuse to do anything or show the results of anything unless it is absolutely perfect. And, in many cases, even if what they have accomplished something amazing, in their eyes, it will never be "perfect" or good enough. This sense of perfectionism can get in the way of hobbies, work, and even relationships. Perfectionism is truly an overbearing burden that does little but hurts and hinders an individual.

Many people especially struggle with this need to be perfect due to the ever-looming audience. This sense of always being watched and judged causes a person to view their faults to an extreme, increasing their self-conscious and self-negative thoughts. The theorist, David Elkind, described how an imaginary audience such as this is detrimental to learning, as it develops a hindrance of perfectionistic tenancies. However, in this day and age, the audience is no longer imaginary. Between the typical school setting with large classes and the online world, which is difficult to escape, people, especially children, always feel the pressure to excel. These environments cause negative comparisons, judgments, and evaluations to arise, and can even lead to bullying in-person and online bullying in many schools. Before long, this pressure leads to anxiety and depression. It is no wonder why children are increasingly feeling the need to present themselves as perfect.

The current school culture, which focuses only on results, is not helping the situation. Instead, teachers and parents should help their students learn to embrace their mistakes rather than avoid them. It may seem odd to embrace mistakes when you want to do well, but there are many ways in which they can help. This may seem contradictory, but if a person doesn't see their mistakes, then they won't know how to grow and improve. They can become stagnant. On the other hand, if a person learns to examine their mistakes, they can then learn how to overcome mistakes, grow, and improve. By repeating this process of regularly examining one's mistakes and then growing, a person can create a habit of being able to accept their mistakes as a beneficial tool for growth.

Sure, an easy A is a great grade for a student, But, this A does not help a student learn how to accept mistakes for growth in the long-run. Often times, students who get easy high grades simply overlook their mistakes and continue along the same path that they always go. This leads to stagnation. Meanwhile, a student who learns to examine their mistakes and grow and continuously grow and excel in life, as they are always excited at the potential to go further and do better.

One way parents and teachers can help is to create an environment where all students are accepted. This means that whether a student gets an F or an A, their effort to learn is accepted and appreciated. They aren't punished for doing poorly. Instead, students are regularly reminded that examining oneself and their mistakes is a wonderful tool for growth. Both types of students, those with high or low grades, are shown their mistakes without shame or punishment. However, when showing the mistakes, it is important to not focus on the seeming "failure," but instead on showing the student how they can overcome the mistake, where they should practice, and showing them their potential. Doing this with all students, regardless of their grades, will help those who score lower feel less shame as they will see it is an ordinary practice that all students go through. This will also help students with high grades to see that even if they are getting an A, they can still grow and go further. That they have a limitless mind and limitless potential if they only put in the effort.

This method does not only apply in the classroom but to the individual, as well. It is easy to hide from your mistakes, refusing to analyze them. To an extreme, a person may even refuse to try, as they assume they will make a mistake, so they don't want to even put in the effort. These habitual negative patterns of thought and action have created neural pathways so that a person is more likely to continue to repeat these behaviors than change. Thankfully, with neuroplasticity, which you learned about in the previous chapter, you can override your previous poor habits and create new pathways with healthier and more positive habits. Through neuroplasticity, even if you have been a perfectionist your whole life, you can learn to overcome these unhealthy tenancies and embrace your mistakes for better growth. I get it; this may seem impossible for someone currently feeling overburdened with their perfectionism. But I promise you that it is possible. Many people, myself included, have overcome their perfectionism for a healthy and happier life that better allows them to understand and overcome their mistakes for growth. You have the power to change your life for the better if you only put in the effort.

A large part of learning to accept and grow from one's mistakes is learning how to accept oneself. By being willing to see yourself as a work in progress, you can then accept mistakes as being a part of that progress. They won't view mistakes a being a threat to their "perfect" identity. As we are all always growing, we will all make mistakes, but choosing to act on these mistakes and grow will allow us to improve throughout life. This is a growth mindset, which will allow a person to excel in all areas of life.

Contrasting the growth-minded person is a fixed-minded person. This person subconsciously believes themselves to be a finished product. The result is that any mistakes they made and are judged for makes them believe that they are permanently subpar or a failure. For instance, if a fixed-minded person is told that a story they wrote is not good enough to be published, they might believe that they will never be capable of writing something to be published. That they fail as a writer. They can become so overwhelmed by their mistakes that they become unable to see their strengths, believing that their story is a complete failure rather than something that has both strengths and weaknesses.

A fixed-minded student will become so overwhelmed, ashamed, and upset by the mistakes that they want to completely avoid them. But, the first step to growth is to examining mistakes so that you can learn from them. By refusing to look as your mistakes, you will only become stagnant. On the other hand, if a person becomes growth-minded, they will have enough self-acceptance to confront their mistakes head-on. They will examine how and why they made a mistake and how they can fix it to grow. Sure, it might not always be pleasant to view one's own mistakes, but with practice, it can become a fun challenge to overcome.

Changing from a fixed mindset to a growth mindset doesn't happen overnight or automatically. It requires consistent practice to engage yourself with your mistakes in all areas of life. Whether the mistake is spilled milk or a bad grade, by being willing to accept and examine your mistakes regularly, it will become a habit and way of life. You must learn to accept yourself mistakes an all, and accept that you failed. Remember, mistakes and failures are not an identity. They don't lock you into being a failure. Instead, they are an opportunity to further yourself and grow.

Greater than the fear and pain of mistakes is that of failure. The difference may seem slim, but it has a great impact on a person's psyche. For instance, mistakes might be getting a B- or your boss, giving you feedback on ways to improve. On the other hand, failure would be getting an F or missing a work deadline. After failing at something, it is even easier to believe oneself to be a failure and become overwhelmed with shame and avoidance. But, just as failure is greater than a mistake, so too is the opportunity to grow. If you fail, you can gain the ability to grow further than you might think possible. The only way to go is up, and you can achieve great things.

The way to deal with failures is slightly different from how you need to deal with your mistakes. While mistakes are typically minor slip-ups or shortcomings, failure reveals a more foundational problem that needs to be addressed. The larger the failure, the more true this statement is. This means that with failure, you not only need to examine and grow from an immediate event but from the root cause, as well.

For instance, if you fail to meet a deadline for school or work, it is likely not due to a single slip-up along the way. Of course, there will always be times that we are unable to succeed due to circumstances out of our control, such as health emergencies, traffic accidents, or family deaths. In this case, you may not return a project in on time, but that was due to circumstances out of your control, and therefore is not counted as a failure in this instance. We are speaking of instances when you should have been able to meet a deadline, but due to a series of mistakes, you failed. This is usually a sign of mistakes during the entire process of the project leading up to the deadline. For instance, you may have frequently made mistakes with a root in time management. Maybe you decided to watch TV or hang out with friends when you should have been working on your project. The root cause could also be procrastination, perfectionism, or even lifestyle addictions.

These failures can be hard to deal with, but it is vital to remember that a failure to succeed in one area of life does not make you as a person as a failure. Remember to keep a growth mindset. These mistakes and failures can help you learn to better yourself at a deep level, benefiting you for years to come. Through this process, you can gain understanding, maturity, and perseverance. Don't allow your failures to get you down to the point where you no longer even try, otherwise you will be unable to improve. Always take these failures as an opportunity to grow and overcome. You can do it if you only put in consistent hard work while examining and overcoming your past mistakes.

If you are a parent or a teacher, you can greatly help a child learn to embrace their mistakes. While many parents and teachers want to be seen as ideal authority figures that don't make mistakes, this only sets a child up for failure. They will see that the adults around them are excelling seemingly without mistakes, and it will set them up with false expectations that will cause them to only beat themselves up more for any mistakes. Thankfully, parents and teachers can easily remedy this by accepting their own mistakes for the child to see. By modeling the proper growth mindset, a child can learn to adopt the behavior, rather than falling into a fixed mindset.

Children don't need a flawless role model that is impossible to achieve. Instead, they need to see that mistakes and failures happen, but it is how we deal with them and grow that truly matters. This role model may be less perfect and more gritty, but it will better help a child grow and learn. Allow a child to see you stumble, fall, and pick yourself back up. That even when you make mistakes, you don't give in to shame and despair.

One powerful way that role models can display a growth mindset is by openly admitting and talking about their own shortcomings. This should be in a curious mindset without judgment. To allow a child to get a full picture of how your growth mindset works, act as if you are a detective examining a crime scene. Examine all the little details, what caused your mistake, and how you can approach the situation in the future to grow and improve. This includes discussing both past and present mistakes. For instance, a present mistake you could discuss with a child is a mistake you made at work, failures in maintaining a healthy lifestyle, and mistakes you have made toward a child themselves. For instance, if you snapped at a child and hurt their feelings, you should be willing to apologize and admit that you made a mistake. You can then explain how you allowed yourself to snap, despite knowing better, and how you plan to improve in the future. Upon seeing this, a child will be more open and willing to embrace a growth mindset, as they will see, adults aren't all talk, promoting one behavior while acting in another.

By promoting a growth mindset by displaying one yourself, you can even improve a child's emotional well-being. This is because of the fear of mistakes and failure are directly linked to a person's self-worth and the value they see in themselves when they have a fixed mindset. Studies have found that children can undergo serious psychological harm due to these behaviors, leading to severe anxiety and depression that can last for years to come. These studies have found that with a growth mindset, children experience less harmful self-blame, actively practiced problem-solving more frequently, and are more likely to respect their teachers.

Now that you understand the importance of a growth mindset to learn, grow, and improve, let's look at six specific benefits you can gain from making mistakes.

1. People Learn from Mistakes

When a person experiences a negative outcome for their work, they are less likely to make the same mistake in the future. By analyzing mistakes and learning from them, you can take a different course of action the next time you deal with a similar situation. Ideally, you can learn from these mistakes with more minor exams and situations so that when you have a more serious exam or situation, you have already learned from your mistake. This is helpful for everyone, children, or adults.

If you are a parent or teacher, it is vital that you

don't try to protect your children from making mistakes. Yes, you should help guide them toward doing things in the right way. But, if you constantly attempt to protect a child from any and every mistake, then they will never learn. This will leave them as adults who never got the chance to learn on their own, and they will then have to learn with more serious matters. Childhood is the perfect time to make simple mistakes on issues that aren't vitally important so that children are prepared for the future.

2. Mistakes Foster Independence and Responsibility

Imagine a child is at school. Their homework is due, but they forgot it at home, which will result in a failing grade. Should the child be allowed to call home and ask their parent to take time away from whatever they have planned for the day to deliver their homework? Or, should the student accept the failing grade? Here's the thing, when children are young, the stakes are usually low. Sure, there are dangers in this world children must be protected from. But, it isn't a parent or teacher's job to protect children from their own mistakes and relatively harmless consequences. When children grow up being sheltered from their own consequences, everyone around them has to pay the price. We see the results of this every day when pampered children grow into adults that take advantage of the weak for their own gain.

Often times, the consequences of the mistakes a child makes will be a poor grade or a reprimand. They don't have to worry about losing their job, going without pay, supporting a family, or going without food. A parent protects them from these serious realities of life while they grow and prepare. And, a large part of being prepared is learning the natural consequences in life. By doing this, children will become more responsible and independent. If they make the mistake of forgetting their homework and getting a failing grade, then they are sure to be more careful about remembering and double-checking their school bag before leaving home in the future. This will translate to greater success when they are an adult.

3. Failure Makes Success More Rewarding

In sports, if a child wins every single game they ever compete in, then they begin to expect success. When they only expect success and never experience defeat, then the success itself begins to lose its meaning. A child will see it as a given and not something worked for and won that they should be proud of. Because of this, they may even begin to become bored with the sport, as it no longer makes them feel excited, passionate, or challenged. However, if a child is continuously experiencing both success and defeat, they will feel challenged and passionate to work harder and improve. When they fail, they will feel the sting of defeat, but this defeat will only push them to grow further. And, when they do experience success, it will feel all the sweeter. There will be nothing better than such a success. Just think about how excited underdog athletes are after a win, you rarely see anything like it!

4. Mistakes Relieve Pressure

When a person is under high pressure to succeed, they naturally make more mistakes and are able to focus less on the task at hand. Just think about the times you have felt anxious about work or school. I'm sure the pressure got to you, messing up your results. This is true for adults and children alike.

Yet, if you know that through making the occasional mistake, you can experience the benefits mentioned in this chapter, then it will take the pressure off. Of course, you will likely still experience some anxiety, but it can be reduced. By reducing this anxiety, you will thereby be able to devote your full ability and brainpower to the task at hand, increasing your chances of success. It will take time to develop this outlook, as you will have to create new neuron pathways through neuroplasticity, but it certainly can be done! If it doesn't help the first time you try this outlook, don't give up, just keep trying every time you have a new task so that you can build those neuron pathways.

When you are undergoing something you are anxious about succeeding in, try telling yourself, "No matter what happens, I can gain something new. If I succeed, then I will have accomplished my mission. If I fail, then I can learn something new to help me in the future."

5. Mistakes Promote Critical Thinking and Problem Solving

If you are a parent or teacher, you are likely aware that it is important to provide children with the ability to develop their problem solving and critical thinking when they are young. These are essential skills for adults, and if children don't develop them before adulthood, they will struggle once they go out into the world as adults. By allowing a child to make mistakes, you help them to learn the skills of problem-solving, critical thinking, and foresight. These children will learn to think for themselves more, such as thinking, "if I do this, then I will experience that consequence." Learning on their own, through their own success and failures, is much more real and believable to a child than having an adult preach at them constantly.

6. Mistakes Improve Memory Retention

It may be surprising to hear, but did you know that mistakes actually improve memory retention? This means if you make mistakes in practice tests, then you are less likely to make mistakes in the actual test. A 2009 study from UCLA proved that people better retain information when they fail to correctly remember it on their first try.

There are many ways you can implement changes to answer questions for information you need to remember, without it affecting your end-goal. For instance, if you or your students have a test or exam coming up, set up practice sessions with other students, coworkers, or even friends and family. These people can quiz you on a series of questions, and any mistakes you make will only help you better retain the information for later. But, even if you do make a mistake in the actual exam, the good news is that you will still remember the information better later on.

As you can see, there are many benefits to changing embracing mistakes and adopting a growth mindset. This change won't happen overnight. But, if you put in the consistent effort, then your neuroplasticity will aid in creating new pathways. Slowly but surely, this growth mindset and openness to mistakes for better learning will become a newly ingrained lifestyle.

CHAPTER 3: CHANGE YOUR MINDSET TO IMPROVE YOUR REALITY

For many people, learning, challenges, and opportunities are fraught with anxiety and worry. Sure, the outcome may bring many good things. But what if you fail? For many of us, we focus more on failure than success, and the anxiety that comes with it brings to mind many thoughts of what could possibly go wrong. Yet, this mindset does nobody any failures. In fact, it only decreases your likelihood of success and makes you miserable along the way. Thankfully, it is possible to change this mindset for one that will bring you great chances of success and joy.

Studies on learning have proven the powerful effects of mindset. While many people may think a positive outlook is cheesy or pointless, the truth is that its effects are well-researched and proven. One such study, by psychologists Stephen Loughnan and Ulrich Weger, studied very matter. In this study, there were two groups of participants. Both groups were expected to answer a series of questions that appeared on a screen. Prior to the question appearing, there would be a brief flash. The first group was told that the flash was the answer to the question, too brief to consciously perceive, but that the unconscious mind would take it in and improve their chances of success. However, the second group was told that this flash was only signaling the next question. The truth? For both groups, the flashes were actually random strings of words and numbers with no meaning. Despite there being no hidden answer in the flashes, the first group experienced much greater success on the test. They were more likely to answer the questions correctly. Not because they had more knowledge, but because they had a more positive mindset and better believed in their ability to answer the questions correctly.

This study, among others, shows that one of the biggest limiting factors we have is the thought itself that we are limited. This means if you believe "I can't do this," or "I'm not capable," then you are limiting yourself more than you know. But, if you remain positive and remind yourself of your abilities, you are capable of increasing your cognitive and physical limits.

You may be able to perceive how a change in

mindset would benefit cognitive abilities, but for many people, it is harder to imagine it improving physical limits, as well. The truth is that by adopting a positive mindset, you can greatly improve your physical limits, which is why so many athletes rely on inspiration quotes to keep their mindset in the right place. A study on this, specifically regarding vision abilities, was conducted in a flight simulator. Since it is commonly believed that fighter pilots have exceptional vision, researchers wanted to see how people would react to being in a flight simulator. In order to create the mindset of an Air Force fighter pilot, the simulator was an actual cockpit with flight instruments set on a hydraulic lift to mimic movement. The people were even given army pilot uniforms to complete the effect. The participants would then sit in the pilot's chair and complete a series of simple maneuvers. While practicing their maneuvers and "flying," they were given a vision test. A control group also practiced flight maneuvers and took the vision test, but this group's cockpit was completely still without the simulator being active. The results? Only the group that had the mindset of a fighter pilot and had the simulator active experienced improved vision. Their vision wasn't naturally better; they simply experienced increased success due to having the right mindset.

The same researchers completed another study on vision and mindset using an eye chart. When using a standard eye chart, the researchers found that people usually read the first two-thirds of the chart, and then struggle to read the last remaining third as the letters get smaller. The researchers then created an altered chart. Instead of the large letters that are typically at the top of the chart, the researchers put the medium-sized font at the top that is usually in the middle of it, slowly progressing to a smaller and smaller font. Because the people believed they could read two-thirds of the chart, as they can with the standard chart, they were able to. This means that they were able to read smaller font than they can on the standard chart, simply because of their mindset.

Your mindset can even affect your weight loss, even if your lifestyle habits remain the same. I may sound impossible, but it has been proven to be true! If you have ever tried to watch your weight, it is likely you have counted your calories, carbohydrates, fats, proteins, or exercise time. But, how much of your time did you focus on a positive mindset? Many people can feel overwhelmed and discouraged when dieting, which is self-defeating. This thought process can actually reduce your likelihood of losing weight, as was shown in a study on physical activity, weight loss, and mindset. In this study, hotel room attendants were examined in two groups—one as a study group, and the other as a control group. This study specifically used hotel room attendants, as on average, they clean fifteen rooms as day with twenty to thirty minutes dedicated to each room. This cleaning meets the recommended thirty minutes of daily exercise to maintain a healthy lifestyle. Despite this, when questioned, most room attendants revealed that they don't believe that they get regular or any exercise at all. The study group was informed that with their work, they meet the recommendation of daily exercise. However, the control group was not told this. During the course of the study, both groups were closely monitored, and none of them changed their diets or exercise habits, either at work or outside of work. Despite everything else staying the same, simply by gaining a bit more information to change their mindset, the study group experienced improvements. Through a study period of four weeks, this group experienced weight loss, body fat loss, improved waist-to-hip ratios, and even lowered systolic blood pressure. During the same course of time, the control group did not see any of these benefits. This goes to show how much mindset can affect the body.

To the layman, physical benefits triggered simply by mindset may sound impossible. But, researchers are all too familiar with the effect of placebos. What is a placebo? It is generally a pill given to a study participant who is told it contains medicine when it is nothing but a fake. These placebos are used in control groups to help researchers understand when a medicine they are testing is truly effective. Or, if it is only having a placebo effect due to the person believing it should work. For instance, researchers have found that placebos can allow people to lift heavier weights, activate the immune system, increase hormone levels, reduce anxiety, and act as an antihistamine. All of this is not due to the placebo itself, but because the human mind believes that the placebo will work, so it makes it so.

Even the most intelligent and capable people can unconsciously sabotage their own success. With daily unconscious negative thoughts, a person can set themselves up for failure. This is known as cognitive distortions. It is normal to have these negative thoughts every now and then, but we must combat them with positive thoughts that improve our mindset. If you have a task to complete, your inner self-critic might be telling you that you will fail. When this happens, many people either refuse to even try, as they see failure as inevitable, or their negative thoughts are a self-fulfilling prophecy. This mindset can do nothing but cause harm. But, if you remind yourself that you can succeed, that even if you make mistakes, they can help you learn, and similar positive thoughts, then you can improve your mindset. Over time, this new positive mindset will become your natural thought process, as neuroplasticity will make it an automatic habit. But, you have to put in the practice and work to overcome your cognitive dysfunctions on a regular basis if you want the help of neuroplasticity.

The first step to overcoming your dysfunctional cognitive thoughts is to realize when you are experiencing them. There are many types of negative self-talk you could be experiencing on an unconscious level. But, by learning about them, you can become more conscious of their existence, allowing you to combat them with a positive mindset. Let's look at the most common cognitive distortions, as found by psychologists.

All-or-Nothing:

With this distortion, you view situations as black-and-white. For instance, if you get a B on an exam or your boss tells you that in one area of a performance review, you don't do that great, then you may believe yourself to be a "complete failure." With this line of thinking, there is no room to recognize where you did do well; you only focus on the negative. You don't see the nuances; you view situations as all-or-nothing. Simply, you view yourself as either successful or a failure, with no in-between. It is much healthier to realize that while yes, you made mistakes, you also succeeded in other areas and have the opportunity to grow.

Mental Filter:

With the mental filter, you may hear a lot of positive encouragement from people, but you filter it out and instead obsess over a single negative or critical detail. For instance, if you hear a critical comment from your teacher or boss, you might filter out all the positive they have to say and only obsess over the criticism.

Overgeneralization:

With the overgeneralization distortion, a person believes that something bad will always happen, simply because it happened once. For instance, if you are assigned to work with another student or coworker you dislike, you don't pass an exam, or you get critical feedback, you might think, "Just my luck! I always fail or get the short end of the stick." This overgeneralization can even cause a person to give up before they even try.

Discounting the Positive:

Many people will reduce their hard work and results buy downplaying any positives regarding a situation or themselves. For instance, even if you do a good job, you will reason with yourself to believe that the job well done wasn't due to anything you did, but other people or circumstances out of your control. This will leave you feeling unfulfilled and as if your actions don't even matter.

Emotional Reasoning:

With emotional reasoning, a person believes that their negative emotions are proof of how true circumstances are. For instance, they may think, "I am terrified of the test coming up. Therefore I must not be prepared and will fail." Or, they might think, "I get nervous whenever I talk with my coworkers, so they must hate me." These thoughts are not based in fact, but rather a person's negative perceptions.

Jumping to Conclusions:

When a person interprets situations negatively without the facts to back up their thoughts, it is jumping to conclusions. With this distortion, a person believes that no matter the facts available, that things will turn out poorly. For instance, before a test or meeting, you might tell yourself, "I'm going to fail."

"Should" Statements:

By using negative "should" statements, a person creates frustration and guilt against themselves and anger and resentment against others. With these statements, a person focuses on how they view a situation how it "should" be, rather than for what it is. For instance, they might think to themselves, "I'm an adult. I should have been able to accomplish this much, as least." When it comes to others, they might think, "My coworkers (or fellow students) should have been able to accomplish this, but they didn't."

Personalization and Blame:

With this cognitive distortion, you personally hold yourself responsible for and blame yourself for situations that aren't entirely under your control. For instance, if your relationship with a coworker or classmate is struggling, you might think, "this is all my fault." However, you should understand that it takes two people to make a situation work, then go from there to pinpoint the exact cause of the problem and do your best to fix it. Another common problem with this distortion is that people can begin to blame any negative circumstance on other people while discounting the ways in which they might be the cause of the problem.

Now that you understand the negative thought patterns that can be caused by cognitive distortions, you may think you can easily overcome them. However, it is easier said than done. Just as a person will naturally look down when someone says, "don't look down," or will think of pink elephants when you tell them not to, it is easier said than done.

Often times, when attempting to overcome negative thoughts, people attempt to distract themselves. But this only lasts for a short time. When the person is once again overcome with the negative thoughts, they begin to beat themselves up for being unsuccessful, only creating even more negative thoughts about themselves. In fact, studies have even found that attempting to overcome such negative thoughts by pushing them away, arguing with them, or drowning them out will only amplify the thoughts and make the situation worse.

Thankfully, with four key practices, you can overcome negative thoughts and create healthier thought pathways. This will allow you to create inner peace and find greater fulfillment and success in life.

Recognize and Remove Yourself from Negative Thought Patterns

Unhelpful thought patterns cause negative emotions such as anxiety, stress, fear, depression, shame, and unworthiness. These cognitive distortions can be overcome with a process of recognizing, identifying, and removing yourself. This process is known as cognitive defusion. With this method, you realize that the thoughts you are struggling with are simply thoughts and nothing else. You learn to take your thoughts, and the negativity they contain, less seriously. You only listen to the thoughts if you find them helpful and positive. Otherwise, you discard them. By understanding that these thoughts simply pass through your mind, you can push them away and make way for more positive thoughts to take their place. This will allow you to overcome their belief and stop the self-fulfilling prophesy that they cause. We have a choice in how we react to our thoughts, and we can choose to turn them into a positive rather than a negative.

Let's have a look at the difference between cognitive fusion (being fused with your thoughts) and cognitive defusion. Imagine that while grabbing coffee first thing in the morning, you have to wait in a long line, only to immediately spill your coffee all over the floor. Now, you may immediately think, "today is just awful," but is this true? Of course not, you simply had a single negative experience; it doesn't have to affect the rest of your day. But, if you choose to believe this negative thought, then you will likely experience a bad day, as it will create a self-fulfilling prophecy.

You don't have to allow yourself to stay fused with the thought that the day is ruined. You can defuse these thoughts for a better mindset. When you experience a thought such as "today is just awful," you can acknowledge the thought, let it go, and instead choose to find and enjoy the good within your day. There are many types of thoughts that this can work on, as you have learned above in the different types of cognitive distortions. But, when you practice overcoming these distortions, it is incredibly liberating.

When you are struggling with these negative thoughts, instead of trying to push them away, try the "name it and tame it," technique. Studies have shown that simply pushing the thoughts away is not only ineffective; it actually amplifies the thought. On the other hand, the name it and tame it technique can help you get these thoughts under control and regain inner peace.

The first step is that when you notice a negative thought pattern and the resulting emotions popping up, name, or label them. You have probably noticed that you regularly struggle with the same cognitive distortion and accompanying thought processes. For instance, you may think, "how could I possibly succeed when I have failed so much in the past?" You can label this thought pattern as the "failure story," and whenever it pops into your mind, say to yourself, "here is the old 'failure' story once again," and then let the thought go.

How do you "let it go?" What I mean by this is that you simply stop taking the thought so seriously, which will then help you give it less of your attention. You begin to realize that it is just a thought and not reality, allowing yourself to see the world and who you are in a more genuine light.

When naming your thoughts, be sure to do so in a kind, gentle, and soothing way. You shouldn't punish yourself or think negatively on yourself for struggling with these thoughts. Instead, be kind to yourself and choose compassion over aggression.

Focus on the Present

When experiencing negative thoughts, they are likely caused by events of the past or the future. This means you are likely dwelling on past mistakes and events, or you are worried about what might happen in the future. These thoughts and emotions can be caused by school, work, finances, relationships, and more. But, when we become engrossed in these negative thought patterns, we tend to lose touch with the present reality. When this happens, we can miss out on the positives and the pleasures of life, coloring our perception of life in light of negativity. We lose touch with not only the world around us but also with ourselves.

But, you can come to your senses and out of your mind by literally focuses on your five senses rather than the thoughts you have been ruminating on. You can practice this no matter where you are—whether it is home, school, work, or even the subway. Focus on using your senses to their absolute fullest and notice all that is going on around you.

A good practice for this technique, known as grounding, is to search for five things you can see, four things you can feel, three things you can hear, two things you can smell, and one thing you can taste. When you do this, there will be little to no room for negative thoughts and excessive rumination. It will calm the mind, allowing you to put things into perspective. Once you complete this technique, you can then try the naming and taming technique, as your mind will be calmer and more able to think rationally.

Helpful Questions

Sometimes, you might find that despite trying the naming and taming technique and the ground technique, you are still struggling with a thought. When that happens, try these helpful questions to aid you with your unhelpful thoughts. These questions will allow you to untangle your thoughts and see the truth more clearly, allowing you to refocus yourself. If simply asking and answering these thoughts mentally doesn't help, then try writing them out or even answering them out loud. Writing and speaking aloud requires more effort and focus, and it can make the process more effective. These questions have helped many people, as they are the same ones used in Acceptance and Commitment Therapy (ACT.)

- Is this thought helpful or useful?
- Do I know without a doubt that it is true?
- Is it simply a habitual thought process my mind plays out of habit?
- Does the thought help me take effective action?
- Is this thought helpful, or simply taking up space in my mind?

After answering these thoughts, you can ask yourself another series of questions to help you refocus and create healthier thought patterns. Again, you can ask these thoughts mentally, out loud, or write them out.

- What is the truth?
- What do I really want to feel or think about in this situation? How can I accomplish my desire?
- What new thought can I focus on now?
- Who could I be without this negative thought?
- How can I make the best of this situation?
- What can I be grateful for at this moment?
- How can I see this in a better way?

These powerful questions will allow you to get out of the negative spiral and create a new positive mindset. With regular and consistent practice, this mindset will become a habit, but you have to put in the effort. You don't dismantle your old neurological pathways and create new ones in a single day. Neuroplasticity is amazing, but it does take regular effort, so don't get discouraged if it takes some time to rewire your brain. In time, you will find that these negative thoughts become less prominent, and the new positive ones will become your new normal.

When you are able to successfully create your new mindset, you will be amazed at your limitless potential. You will find that you are capable of doing more, whether your goal is cognitive or physical. These benefits can be experienced in every area of your life, transforming it for the better.

CHAPTER 4: OPEN-MINDEDNESS IS THE KEY TO LEARNING

Frequently, people are taught a single way to learn. But, if that method doesn't work for them, they can begin to feel "dumb" or inadequate. While this can affect anyone, it can especially affect those with learning disabilities, such as dyslexia. But, if you focus on learning—or teaching your struggling students—multidimensional practices with open-mindedness, then you can experience success like never before.

With a multidimensional approach to learning, you can develop new ways to tackle problems. By being able to see a situation in a new way, you can then develop strategies that work better to find the correct answer with less struggle. Let's look at an example of how a person might use multidimensional thinking. This example uses a child, but it applies to people of all ages.

Imagine that a child has a set of one-hundred flashcards. Each of the cards has either a dog, a rabbit, or a bird. They are also categorized by color, either blue, green, or red. When a child is given these flashcards, they might sort them by either color or animal. This means that they can see two different ways to approach sorting the cards, rather than a single method. Being able to switch methods of sorting shows that a child has multidimensional thinking and is able to remain flexible.

However, young children might struggle with this multidimensional thinking. Due to their young brains that haven't fully developed yet, they will insist that there is only one way to sort the cards. They might choose to only sort them by color. Even when an adult encourages them to sort the flashcards by animal, the child might become confused or overwhelmed, unsure how to switch gears to complete the task. If this continues as a child gets older, it could show that the child struggles with multidimensional thinking.

There are three main executive skills, which people typically develop as they age. These are working memory, self-control, and flexible thinking. When these three skills are combined, a child is able to better manage their thoughts, emotions, and actions. If even one of these executive skills is missing, the child will struggle, and this struggle will continue into adulthood if they don't learn ways to manage or learn these skills.

You can easily see how these three skills are used just to solve a simple math problem. Self-control is vital in order to stay focused on the task at hand. Working memory is used so that a person can remember the formulas they have learned and apply them to the math problem. And, flexible thinking is used to consider possible alternative ways to solve the problem if the first attempt failed.

If a person struggles with multidimensional—or flexible—thinking, they likely also struggle with the other two executive skills, as they are deeply entwined in the brain. But, this doesn't mean that the person will experience the same level of struggle for each of the skills; they may struggle more in one area than the other two.

If you suspect you or a child is struggling with these executive skills, testing can be done to diagnose if there is a problem and to find exactly where the person is struggling. Once you know the exact problem, then it is easier to create support and tools to help the person better succeed. There are many learning disorders and differences that can cause these troubles. One of the most common is Attention Deficit Hyperactivity Disorder (ADHD) But, the only way to know what is causing difficulties is to be evaluated by an expert. No matter a person's age, whether a child or adult, they can be evaluated. This is highly recommended, as this evaluation will greatly help a person understand themselves and how to combat their struggles.

There are many different ways multidimensional thinking can be used in daily life. In the examples below, we will be using children as an example so that parents and teachers can better recognize any struggles their children might be experiencing. However, I know that these issues also affect adults. In fact, limited multidimensional thinking will cause even more problems for adults than children, as it is a necessary aspect of daily life. As an adult supporting yourself, rather than relying on parents, these struggles will become increasingly apparent.

1. Multidimensional Thinking and Learning

Multidimensional thinking, also known as cognitive flexibility, requires two unique skills, which are flexible thinking and set-shifting. A person uses flexible thinking when they think about a situation or circumstance in a new way. They then practice set-shifting when they let go of their old method of action to adopt the new method.

One example of how these two skills form together to create multidimensional thinking is by apologizing. If a child starts out apologizing by always shifting blame, saying, "I'm sorry you didn't like what I did," or "I'm sorry your ornament broke so easily," a child can be taught to apologize in a better way. An adult can teach them to instead apologize without shifting blame by taking responsibility for their own actions. These apologies can switch to being "I'm sorry that I hurt your feelings," and "I'm sorry I broke your ornament." With this example, the child uses flexible thinking to consider the new approach presented to them. They then use set-shifting to unlearn their old method and adopt the new method.

When children struggle with multidimensional thinking and are rigid; instead, they will struggle to learn new basic ways of doing things. This does not only apply to apologizing but many aspects of daily life. It could deal with how to tie shoelaces, pet cats, do house chores, and more. If a child exhibits struggles with multidimensional thinking in a variety of everyday circumstances, it can be difficult for them to take on new responsibilities and tasks as they age.

2. Multidimensional Thinking and Reading

When a child is learning to read, they have to use multidimensional thinking to understand how the process works. It can be difficult, as even the same letter combinations can make different sounds depending on the word. For instance, the letter combination "ough" sounds different in the word "enough" than in the word "dough." The same words can also be used in different ways, such as the word "slip" in the phrases "sign the permission slip" and "don't slip on the banana peel."

Even after a child learns to read, they can still struggle as they use books to learn information. When reading, they require multidimensional thinking to understand which information in the book is helpful information and what is unimportant. Similarly, multidimensional thinking is used to understand different character perspectives in a story, idioms, and puns.

If your child is overly rigid in their thinking, then they may show it by having trouble pronouncing words, interpreting what they read too literally, or becoming confused by puns and idioms.

3. Multidimensional Thinking and Writing

Writing is a complicated process for children and adults alike. However, it is especially difficult for children who have less experience. In this case, they can struggle to know how to properly organize their thoughts and form them into coherent sentences. While doing this, they have to keep many other aspects in mind, as well. For instance, they also need to be able to focus on the main topic while adding in supporting details; checking to see if their grammar is correct; and ensure that they have used all the right spelling. All of these processes require multidimensional thinking, as a rigid thinker will struggle to balance and shift thought processes between all the different elements.

A child may show overly rigid thinking in their writing by having little supporting detail, confusing sentences, or excessive errors.

4. Multidimensional Thinking and Language Learning

With multidimensional thinking, a person can learn

the rules of a language, whether it is their native language or an additional language. For instance, it helps them know how to put words into the past tense. In English, we frequently use "ed" at the end of a word to signal past tense, for instance, you might say that a person is "scrubbing the dishes," if they are currently cleaning. On the other hand, if you are talking in the past tense, you could say they "scrubbed the dishes." While a multidimensional thinker is able to realize that there are exceptions to this rule, such as with "fly" and "flew," rigid thinkers will struggle with this and try to use "ed" at the end of all words used in the past tense.

Flexible thinking is especially important when learning a second language, as a person will have to learn that other languages have different structures, sounds, and rules. These aspects can be difficult to learn for anyone when they are used to speaking a single language, but it is especially difficult for rigid thinkers.

A rigid thinker may find it difficult to learn language rules and exceptions. Because of this, they are likely to learn better by listening to a person speaking a language in everyday conversation rather than reading in a book.

5. Multidimensional Thinking and Math

Multidimensional thinking is even an important skill in math. For instance, a person uses this skill to determine what a written math question means. If the question uses the phrase "how many in all," the child can use this skill to help them realize that the question indicates the problem is addition. They can also use multidimensional thinking to realize that there is more than one way to solve a math problem. If one formula doesn't work, then they can try a new method.

Without strong, multidimensional thinking, a person can struggle to solve more than a few math questions at a time. They may give up on confusing problems without an answer.

6. Multidimensional Thinking and Studying

Even studying requires multidimensional thinking. Kids need to know how to switch between their different school subjects to accomplish all their studying before school deadlines. Otherwise, they will run out of time. This becomes increasingly apparent as a child ages and is given more homework. A child must be able to switch from completely different subjects, from math to writing assignments. This can be difficult, as both subjects require completely different approaches.

When studying, multidimensional thinking is important to understand which information to focus on. For example, what information do they need to memorize or solve? Or, do they need to learn how to grasp a concept and then retell it in their own words for an essay?

If a child doesn't have multidimensional thinking, then it can be difficult to switch between subjects, leading to frustration.

While the examples we used on multidimensional thinking focus on children, the truth is that this is an important cognitive skill for children and adults alike. For instance, in the workplace, a person might use these skills to solve problems creatively, learn quickly, think flexibly, and adapt to new situations without delay. Because of this, studies have found that more companies are hiring based on a person's cognitive ability through multidimensional thinking. In fact, nine of the top fifteen industries in the world, according to the 2016 World Economic Forum, are prioritizing hiring employees with higher multidimensional thinking capabilities. This shows that whether you are a child or an adult, whether you are in school or the workforce, it is important to improve your multidimensional thinking. But, is it possible to improve this ability, or is it simply something you are born with? The good news is that while some people may be born with impaired multidimensional thinking due to learning disabilities, everyone has the power to improve their ability! With simple methods, you can improve your multidimensional thinking, and thus your potential.

Now, let's look at some simple daily steps you can take to improve your multidimensional thinking, regardless of age.

Fluctuate Your Daily Routine

A simple way you can begin improving your multidimensional thinking is by changing your routine up and trying new things on a regular basis. For instance, if you usually eat the same meal for lunch, change it up, and try making or buying something you wouldn't usually eat. If you always take the same route to school or work, try to find a new route. If you usually exercise at the same park, try exercising in a different location. If you usually go running in the evenings, try riding a bike or using skates.

While these may be simple changes, they can have quite an effect on a person's cognitive abilities. Even smaller changes, such as moving the furniture in your house or using your non-dominant hand for a specific task, can help you strengthen your neural pathways building your multidimensional thinking.

Search For New Experiences

Whenever you learn something new or experience something you usually wouldn't, the neurons in your brain create new synaptic connections. These connections improve neuroplasticity and multidimensional thinking. These interesting and new experiences have even been shown to improve motivation, learning, memory, and mental well-being by releasing dopamine—otherwise known as the happiness hormone. This means that if you actively search out new and interesting experiences, engaging in what you usually wouldn't, you can greatly improve your multidimensional abilities.

There are many ways you can search out new experiences. While most people may think of traveling, this is a more expensive option. You can also try volunteering, exploring a part of town or the countryside that you are unfamiliar with, learning a language or instrument, or taking a class to learn another new skill.

Practice Creative Thinking

Actively practicing to think in unconventional and creative ways can help a person strengthen their cognitive abilities and multidimensional thinking. After all, you won't improve if you don't practice. In one study conducted by psychologist Dr. Robert Steinberg, it was found that simply by practicing these skills, you can greatly strengthen them. In this study, students were taught not only how to think in practical ways, but also in creative ways. The result was that the student's grades improved and they were able to utilize the creative thinking skills they learned in other areas of life, as well.

Usually, multidimensional thinking occurs when a person sees circumstances as having unlimited possibilities, rather than a closed option of choices. This promotes spontaneity and free-flowing thought.

There are many ways to practice creative thinking. To do this, simply try to see situations as limitless and look for new ways to solve problems or in how you go about a situation. This can apply to anything from math to cooking.

One simple exercise you can do is to draw thirty circles on a blank piece of paper. Once the circles are drawn, set a timer for three minutes and fill in as many of the circles with simple sketches as you can in the time limit. This will workout your creative "muscles," the same as lifting weights for your actual muscles would. If you practice this skill periodically, you will notice that your creativity improves overtime and find weaknesses that hold you back.

Take The More Difficult Approach

We all have a lot going on in life. This leads us to often taking the easiest approach to meet our needs, whether it is using a GPS instead of looking at a map, ordering takeout rather than cooking our own meals, or using autocorrect rather than manually correcting writing errors. While these easy options are certainly helpful and have their place, by always relying on them, we are only hindering our cognitive abilities.

Studies have proven that if we choose to take the more difficult route when we are able, we can improve multidimensional thinking and keep our minds sharp. This allows you to learn through your everyday experiences in a controlled manner. For instance, you may choose to take an easy approach if you are having a busy or difficult day. But, on a good day, you can choose to take the difficult approach and stretch your multidimensional thinking muscles.

For instance, instead of relying on a calculator, you can try doing a quick formulation with paper and pen. If you don't trust your ability, you can always double-check the result afterward with a calculator, but this will allow you to stretch those muscles. You can also try navigating an area with a map, rather than your GPS.

Transfer What You Have Learned

By learning something and then transferring what you gained to a new situation or context, you can learn to think more flexibly, thereby improving your multidimensional thinking. This is because it forces your neurons to create new connections between your knowledge pathways. For instance, if you have knowledge pathways for additional languages and for writing, you could create a connection between the two by practicing writing in one of your additional languages.

If you are unable to or don't practice, transferring knowledge to a variety of skills and contexts, your learning will be limited. This learning will also have less impact on your neural connections and multidimensional thinking. In fact, one study found that while children who have been abandoned and lived on the street were able to utilize complex mathematical equations for selling wares and making a living, this knowledge didn't transfer to other contexts. Once the children were taken care of and placed in school, they struggled to transfer the same knowledge to the context of studying and tests in school.

Studies have found that one great way to practice transferring knowledge is to explain the research you have learned in your own words. This can help you to generalize the concepts behind the knowledge, as well as identify any of your incorrect assumptions. Once you have fully understood the information, practice applying it in a variety of real-world situations.

Challenge Your Morals

There are many benefits to challenging your morals. Frequently, people stand firmly in their beliefs regarding socio-political and religious matters. While it is certainly okay to stand by your beliefs and morals, it can become deeply troubling if a person refuses to challenge their morals, listen to the opposition, and heed any warnings. On the other hand, studies have shown that if you seek out experiences that test these morals, you can gain a better understanding of other people's and culture's experiences. This naturally leads to more flexible and multidimensional thinking.

Even if you don't agree with another person's beliefs or point of view, with multidimensional thinking, you will be able to better understand where they are coming from. This will improve not only your multidimensional thinking, but also your understanding of other people, understanding of yourself, and your compassion. Naturally, this will improve your communication skills, allow you to adapt your thinking to a variety of circumstances, and resolve conflicts.

Of course, these are only a few ways to improve your multidimensional thinking. In later chapters, we will go into more details on ways you can create a limitless mind both inside and outside the classroom.

CHAPTER 5: STAY FLEXIBLE; DON'T GET STUCK IN PRECONCEIVED IDEAS

One common preconceived idea is that people who learn quickly and remember well are smarter. It's understandable why people would feel this way, especially if a person struggled with memory themselves and was jealous of those with quick memorization skills. But, the truth is that while memory can affect the speed of learning, it doesn't affect a person's intelligence or capability to learn. It is time to get away from this preconceived notion and flexibly embrace the reality: you can learn.

Working memory is a large factor in the speed at which a person learns. To better understand this skill, and how you can improve it, let's look at several different ways you can use working memory in daily life.

One aspect that working memory affects is accessing stored memory. Of this, there are two types of working memory—auditory and visual-spatial. In effect, stored memory works much like recording a video. You have the actual visible footage, which is the visual-spatial memory. Then, you have what you can hear on the footage, which is the auditory memory. Sadly, unlike real video footage, you are unable to replay stored memory back whenever you want. At least, not completely accurately. You may remember fragments, but you are unlikely to remember a conversation word-for-word or every detail that you were able to see at the time. In fact, working memory is a type of memory "file," to keep with the footage comparison, that quickly becomes corrupted if not used immediately. This means that it is a short-term memory, rather than long-term.

With working memory, you have to focus on exact details you want to remember while they are happening, actively working on remembering them. For instance, if a teacher or parent is explaining math formulas and problems to a child, the child has to use working memory to remember what the person is explaining so that they can then act on it and solve the math problems. If a person has weak working memory, then they will have a difficult time holding onto new information as they see and hear it. The result is that they have a more difficult time solving the problem, as they are unable to accurately remember the information.

If a person has learned mathematical formulas and has it stored in their long-term memory, then they may be able to accurately complete a variety of calculations. But, if the math problems are word-based, they may have difficulty listening and understanding the exact words used. They might not be able to accurately grab the keywords in the phrase, making it difficult to understand the problem.

Working memory is required for remembering instructions as they are given; this is especially difficult if a person is given multiple instructions or multi-step instructions. This is because the more information they are given, the more that they are likely to forget rather than storing in their working memory. While many people will look back on the conversation to remember what instructions they were given, this is difficult for a person with weak working memory. They may forget only snippets of the instructions, or they may even forget most of it, depending on how weak their working memory is. Often times, these people prefer to be given written instructions, so that they can read over the instructions whenever they need to, rather than relying on their weak memory.

Do you find yourself struggling to focus and pay attention in many situations, even when you desperately want to and are trying your best? The truth is that working memory is responsible for your ability to concentrate and focus. This means that if your ability to focus is weak, your working memory likely is, as well. But, it also means that if you strengthen your working memory, then you can also strengthen your ability to focus. One great example of working memory in this context is when a person is doing a long division mathematical problem. During the process, not only does the person need to figure out the correct answer, but they also need to focus on each step along the way. People with weak working memory may struggle with staying on a single task until its completion.

Children with weak working memory will likely struggle to learn to read. A person needs visual-spatial working memory to remember what letters and words look like, allowing them to recognize them in a sentence. They also need auditory working memory to sound out new words that they haven't yet learned. When a person's working memory is strong, they can sound out words that they see with less hesitation. This helps them to become fluent readers more quickly and easily than a person with weak working memory. For kids with weak working memory, learning to read can be a difficult and stressful process that requires a lot of hands-on care and encouragement from the adults around them.

Lastly, let's look at how working memory can work in the active process of learning math. The process of learning math requires many stepping stones that allow a person to slowly complete more complex problems. One of the most important stepping stones in this process is the ability to recognize and reproduce important formulas and patterns. This step allows a person to recognize the patterns in numbers so that they can then solve basic problems. Once children are able to remember and build up this knowledge, they begin to remember mathematical formulas, both simple and complex. But, these stepping stones of learning math require visual-spatial working memory. If a person's working memory is weak, then it can be difficult to build up these stepping stones and learn mathematical formulas. Of course, this isn't to say it's impossible; it simply takes more time and effort. Thankfully, there are ways to can practice to actively strengthen your working memory.

Often time, people believe that 'slow' means 'unintelligent.' But this is not the case. After all, a person's intelligence is comprised of many different cognitive skills, abilities, knowledge, and more. The speed of processing information is only a single aspect of learning, and it does not impact a person's intelligence. Labeling a person as unintelligent because they are a slow learner or have a learning disability is simply unfair discrimination.

Don't believe me? Many studies have been done to test the speed of learning and its impact on intelligence, and these studies have found no consistent link between the two. These studies have concluded that slow learners are not necessarily any less intelligent than quick learners. In fact, some studies have even found that as slow learners take more time to process information deeply, it allows them to remember the information learned more accurately in the future. For instance, rather than cramming before an exam and then quickly forgetting the information once the exam is complete, slow learners can remember and utilize the information for years down the road. Similarly, another study found that even if it takes a person longer to complete an exam than other participants, on average, they are not likely to score lower than their peers.

One study showed that if students are forced to slow down when learning, they can actually learn better. This was accomplished by giving students information written in a difficult-to-read font. This font made the students read more slowly. But, because they were forced to slow down, later on, they were better able to recall the information than that learning with a traditional easy-to-read font. Remember, while you may want to improve your learning speed if you have a weak working memory, know that speed itself is not a part of having a limitless mind. If you truly want to absorb information and excel, you must find a balance so that you can learn steadily while also fully absorbing the information.

Let's look at some examples of quick and slow learning, both efficient and inefficient.

Fast and Ineffective:
One of the most popular methods of fast and ineffective learning is cramming. With this method, people will try to study as much as they can for hours

on end. They will often memorize just barely enough of a given subject to do well on the exam. Often times, this includes skimming books to quickly absorb what little information you can. However, this learning method only allows you to partially grasp onto the knowledge, not fully absorbing it at a deep level. It may help you pass an exam, but the knowledge likely won't stick with you for long after the exam ends. As the information was only learned partially at a surface level, you won't be able to rely on accessing it again in the future.

Slow and Ineffective:

The most common method of slow and ineffective learning is simply not getting 'it.' Go to any place of learning, and you are likely to see people struggling with this. They may have taken Spanish classes for several years, but only remember the most basic of phrases and are hopeless when it comes to holding a conversation. Maybe they have put in hundreds of hours in a given class, but they can hardly remember the information only a few short years later. There are many causes that lead to this poor learning method. It could be that the teacher gives poor instruction and doesn't offer to answer questions or help the students alone. Maybe the students are unmotivated. Or, perhaps the students don't know techniques for how to learn well. If the last case is true for you, then by learning the techniques in this book, you, too, can gain a limitless mind.

Fast and Effective:

Known as ultra learning, this is a style of rapid-learning that focuses on gaining the knowledge at a deep level so that it can be retained and remember for long to come. That's not to say this type of learning is easy. It is one of the most difficult methods and not necessarily more effective or efficient than other types. A couple of types of ultra learning include the Year Without English and the MIT Challenge, but there are more, as well.

Slow and Effective:

One of the best methods of learning is patient mastery. It may not be the quickest method, but it allows a person to effectively learn and master whatever they set their mind to. This is done by slowly studying and gaining knowledge, along with practicing habits. This method is all about the process of learning, practicing effective habits while avoiding stagnating in your routine.

If I were to recommend one style of learning, it would be patient mastery, as it is best suited to individuals and increases success. Of course, if you can find a balance between patient mastery and speed of learning, that is best. The goal of this book is to allow this type of learning. By following the methods and recommendations in this book, you should be able to strengthen your brain and gain this ability.

The truth is that there are benefits both to slow learning and quick learning. For instance, when slow learning is conducted effectively, it allows a person to gain the spacing effect. This is beneficial, as studies have found that by spreading out the time of learning and study, a person is able to improve their long-term retention and memory of the knowledge. Meaning, if you spend one hour a day learning a given subject for an entire week, rather than spending one day studying for seven hours, you are likely to retain the information better. You may be spending the same amount of time studying, but this slow method is more effective for long-term use. In this sense, slow learning has an advantage over quick learning. In fact, even studying for fewer hours over a long stretch of time can provide better long-term retention than studying for longer sittings rapidly.

You should also consider how easily accommodating learning methods are in your lifestyle. It is generally easier to study for short periods daily rather than spending most of your day studying. You can more easily fit a couple of hours of studying in your week, than ten or more hours. If a person believes that they have to use rapid learning, then they can believe that they don't have time to study, as they can't put a lot of time into it. But, even with a limited amount of time, you can still learn a new subject to greater effect if you go at a slower pace.

Of course, this isn't all to say that quick learning is void of benefits. We are all aware that learning quickly has its own benefits—such as saving time. When done correctly, speedy learning can be effective, too! For instance, while the full-immersion method for language learning is difficult, it is also generally much quicker and effective than learning through textbooks or in a classroom setting. This is why many people choose to temporarily travel to or move to a country that speaks their target language, despite the cost of moving.

Sometimes it is helpful to start out with a more rapid learning pace, which you can slowly reduce over time. This allows you to see results quickly so that your motivation doesn't fade over time. Once you begin to see these results and have the motivation to keep going, to can reduce the learning pace to one that more easily fits into your regular lifestyle.

Now, it's important to note that there are multiple factors that affect working memory and learning speed. Because of this, you might notice that at certain points in your life, you are able to confidently and enthusiastically learn at a balanced speed. But, at other times, you might find that your learning speed is diminished, and you have a difficult time picking things up.

Anyone can relate to stress during the learning process. This is because the academic and workplace settings often promote stress, as a person feels pressured to succeed and come out on top. Even if you are a person who doesn't let academic pressure get to you, stress from outside events in life can affect your overall stress level while learning. The good news is that short terms of low-level stress can improve learning! But, chronic or excessive stress causes a backfire.

Stress has been shown to affect the formation of new memories. It is more difficult to learn when stressed, as it impedes the formation of short-term memories, and thus long-term memories, as well. Stress can also color our memories of an event, making us believe things played out differently than they actually did. Lastly, memories can change over time. Each time we mentally review a memory, we will slightly alter it based on our present state of mind. Whenever we revisit this memory, we can make slight unconscious alterations, until we can remember an event completely wrong. As you can see, stress has quite an effect on our memories, which naturally translates to how we learn.

The good news is that studies have found that if stress is directly linked to the information you are learning, such as stress caused by academics, you are more likely to form a memory of the information. Although, if the stress is caused by an outside source, such as something in your personal life, you are less likely to remember the material. It is also important to mention that stress leads to cognitive exhaustion, which will impair focus and working memory.

What does all this mean? To put it simply, to improve your working memory and focus, it is best to reduce your lifestyle stressors. Try to study when you are well rested with minimal stress. But, if you have mild to moderate stress related to learning the subject, it can actually improve learning if it does not become excessive.

If you find stress is getting to you and impeding your learning speed, there are some methods you can use to lower your stress. But, these methods not only reduce stress, but they also improve overall learning, helping to get you to your goal of having a limitless mind!

Whenever you find yourself feeling stress and weighed down, get moving with some aerobic exercise. In one study, participants who were struggling with impaired memory caused by chronic stress exhaustion enrolled in a twelve-week exercise program. These participants experienced great improvement in their stress, memory, and cognitive abilities.

In another study, it was found that participants who experienced impaired memory, reduced learning speed, and stress also frequently suffer from lack of sleep. If you remember from earlier in this book, we went into detail on how sleep is vital for learning, and being sleep deprived will greatly reduce ones learning ability. But, the study also found that the participants who regularly practice mindfulness exercises experienced less stress, improved sleep, and fewer memory impairments.

It is commonly recommended to learn and actively practice breathing exercises and techniques. In fact, many mindfulness techniques will recommend pairing the technique with a breathing exercise for optimal benefits. In one study, it was found that by incorporating breathing exercises in police cadet training, participants were able to improve psychological performance and improve memory recall to boost learning. In the study, it was found that the most benefits were experienced when the cadets paired breathing exercises with focus and positive visualization of gaining success.

Lastly, as much of stress in the academic world is based on a desire to do well and succeed, it can help to train yourself to think more optimistically. Remember, we discussed earlier in this book that embracing mistakes can decrease stress. After all, mistakes help us to learn, so they are a great opportunity. But, if you allow yourself to focus on your mistakes in a negative way, instead of a positive way, you will increase your stress. If this stress gets out of hand, it can reach the point where it impedes working memory increases a person's chances of making mistakes. Practice replacing your neurological pathways of negative self-talk, with optimistic self-talk. This means that whenever you catch yourself thinking negatively about the learning experience or yourself, you should stop the thought and reframe it into something positive. By doing this consistently, neuroplasticity will allow you to create new optimistic pathways so that it becomes a regular way of life that you do without effort.

As you can see, there are many benefits to slower

learning. While we may want to learn as quickly as possible, it is important to stay flexible and challenge our preconceived notions. By utilizing a slower learning process a majority of the time, you can enable yourself to learn at a deeper and more reliable level. You can then complement these periods of slower learning with the occasional quick-learning sessions, to reach optimal success.

CHAPTER 6: FAVORING CONNECTIONS TO BOOST POTENTIAL

While things aren't always easy breezy when you are trying to learn as a group, there are many benefits to group study and learning. In this chapter, we will discuss the pros of studying alone vs. in a group, and how to go about studying as a group effectively.

First, let's look at the pros of studying alone. Many people prefer studying on their own, as it offers fewer distractions, allowing them to focus completely on the reading material. This can be especially true of people who are easily distracted. There is no worry that the study session will turn into simply hanging out and talking or playing. They know that their goal is, and they can accomplish it without the worry of interference.

Every person has their own method of preparing for a test and a certain environment that works well for them. Maybe the like to work at a coffee shop, in the library, or in their bedroom with music. Some people require a space with no distractions, whereas others may work better with ambient noise and people moving around. It all depends on a person's specific personality and cognitive needs; no one way is superior. When studying alone, you are able to meet these needs, as you don't have to account for a group.

Lastly, when you are studying alone, you are fully in control of the schedule. You don't have to worry about scheduling studying around other peoples' schedules and commitments. You don't have to worry about curfews. You don't have to worry about giving up a time of day you would rather spend doing something else because it works better for the group at large. It can be difficult to find a time that works for everyone when studying in a group, and the larger the group, the more difficult it is. But, studying alone gives you the freedom to study whenever you want and for however long you want.

Now, let's look at the benefits of studying in groups. Even if you can't handle studying in a large group, I recommend studying at least occasionally in a small group of two to three people. This will give you the benefits of group study, with fewer potential drawbacks.

When students have the opportunity to discuss concepts with each other during the study process, they are able to help each other understand whether or not they have fully comprehended the study material. Not only can other students who have a better grasp of the material help explain any confusion, but any questions that are asked of the group will give a child the opportunity to think and answer. This opportunity is a wonderful opportunity for learning; whether they are correct or incorrect, as either way, they will make learn and deepen the correct answer in their cognitive pathways.

It can be frustrating to study material that you have trouble grasping. For instance, if a child has a weakness in math, it can be difficult to go to studying alone with nobody to answer questions. But, in a group setting, students stronger in math can help those weaker in the subject. Ideally, students can trade-off helping each other. For instance, one strong in math but weak in history can help another that is weak in math but strong in history, and vice versa.

There are many students, especially extroverts, that have trouble getting motivated to study on their own. They simply can't sit still and focus when they need to recharge and be around people. But, by studying in a group, these students can get what they need. Even if all they are doing is studying and learning, without any casual conversation, it can still benefit an extrovert to be around other people. Not only that but having other students around who are focused on learning will help hold the child accountable, as positive peer pressure encourages them to go along with the group and study, as well. Often, children won't want to be a negative factor of the group, so they will go along with studying without complaint. Of course, this only works if the group is focused on studying.

It's all too easy to procrastinate, for children and adults alike! Whenever there is a deadline, people have a tenancy to put off the work with a deadline, and instead distract themselves with household chores, video games, or hanging out with friends. But, study groups have a specific meeting time and purpose. Because of this, a student can't procrastinate showing up and studying in the same way that they were alone. Imagine, if you are alone it's easy to make an excuse and say "I'll just watch a little more TV before I study," that is until it's too late and you have to go to sleep. It's different if you are in a study group because everyone knows the purpose of the study group. You won't show up and watch TV or play video games; you simply have to get down to business and get your studying done.

When you are studying alone, you always see the material from your own limited perspective. Every person has their own perspective based on their circumstances, and it is hard to see outside of this perspective unless we actively practice. By studying in a group, each student can share their own perspective, helping all students learn from each other and understand the material on a more thorough level. As they discuss the matter, ask questions, and listen, students will develop critical thinking skills that will serve them well throughout life.

When students study together, they can often learn more quickly than they could on their own. This is for multiple reasons. First, because rather than getting stuck on problems, they can help one another solve them with less delay. Secondly, learning as a group offers the potential to promote neuroplasticity and stronger cognitive pathways as you are actively talking through problems, discussing them, making mistakes, and fixing your mistakes. All of these together allows you to learn more quickly.

Lastly, teamwork is very important. Whether you are working one-on-one in a team of two or in a large group, you have to actively practice teamwork. This is a valuable skill that will serve you well, not only in school but also in the workforce and your private life with your relationships. After all, long-term relationships can not be maintained without teamwork. Even if you don't like working in groups, it is likely your teacher, professor, parent, or boss will require you to work as part of a team from time to time. It is simply an aspect of life we can not avoid if we are to live as a member of society. If you want to do well on your exams and get your dream job, then you need to hone this skill. And, you can not hone a skill without practice. Group study sessions are the perfect opportunity to hone your abilities to work within the group effectively.

It's easy to see that there are many benefits to studying in groups, whether big or small, occasionally or regularly. But how do you create an ideal study group? Don't worry; we have some easy steps you can follow, whether you are studying in compulsory school, higher education, or for the workforce.

First, you should consider how many people your study group should contain. If you are an introvert or get easily distracted with other people around, then you should consider a small group of two to three people, yourself included. But, regular group size recommendation is four to six people. This site is great, as it is just large enough to include a variety of strengths and weaknesses and perspectives while minimizing distractions. With this number of people, you can also reduce the risk of unnecessary socialization, lower the number of people talking over one another, and maximize full participant contribution so that everyone gets what they need out of the group.

When choosing your participants, you want everyone to share a common goal, such as passing a given exam. This will ensure everyone wants the same thing out of the study group, and everyone is studying the same material so that you can help each other and discuss the material as a group. It is often best to choose individuals with unique strengths so that you can all fill in for each other's weaknesses. You should also take into consideration people's personalities and relationship dynamics so that everyone who you have together gets along. For instance, if you know two individuals always fight, then you don't want to invite both of them to be a part of your study group, as it will only cause conflict and stress.

It is best to study in a place that is free from distractions, but where you are allowed to communicate and discuss the material freely. A popular cafe would be too crowded and distracting, but if you know of a quiet cafe that has a slow period during specific times, then that could work. However, generally, somebody's home or a library study room is the ideal location. Study rooms at libraries can be reserved, they are quiet, free of distractions, don't cost anything, and you can discuss the study material in them as the room is separated from the rest of the library.

Even if everyone has the day off, you shouldn't schedule study groups to be an all-day event. Remember, breaks are important. If your study session is too long, people will get stressed, tired, hungry, distracted, and the productivity of the learning itself will be diminished. Because of this, you shouldn't schedule study sessions to be any longer than two to three hours in length. Remember, the longer the session, the more likely people are to chat and waste time. It has been found that less time is wasted with poorly timed socializing when study sessions or an hour or less in length.

When you plan your group study for will entirely depend on the schedule of everyone participating. But, if you are hosting a regular study session, such as a weekly event, then it is best to create a specific day and time you all meet every week. For instance, if everyone knows that Tuesdays at 4 pm is set aside for the study group, they will avoid scheduling anything else for that time slot. This can delay having back-and-forth debates every session about when the next session should be held.

Prior to starting the study session, you should elect someone that is patient but good at keeping everyone under control as the leader of the group. While the group should listen to all voices, it will mainly be the leader's job to stop rambling conversations, distractions, keep everyone on task, and ensure everyone gets to participate. There are many people, particularly those who are reserved or introverted, who struggle to participate in a group setting. The leader should be someone who can quiet down those who talk over the introverted members while encouraging the quiet members to speak up.

You should set a clear goal prior to a session so that everyone knows what to work on. It is best to set this goal ahead of time so that everyone is prepared. For instance, this will allow students to bring specific resources, textbooks, and notes that they might have stored at home depending on what specific material you will be studying.

There are many benefits to studying in groups. Even if your group is small, there are still benefits to be had. Try to find people with similar goals to study with, and you are sure to see your learning progress.

CHAPTER 7: USING THE KEYS TO UNLIMITED LEARNING ON YOUR OWN

Throughout this book, we have discussed how many many different elements are interconnected to affect learning. In this chapter, we will examine some of the ways you can use these keys to learning to improve your success and gain an unlimited mind. A few of these might have been mentioned elsewhere in the book, but are included here so that you can conveniently come back to reference and refresh yourself on this chapter time and again as you seek to improve your learning experience.

Of course, the information in this chapter and the next can not replace the wealth of information that precedes these chapters, so remember to read this book again whenever you find yourself hitting a wall.

Speak Key Points Out Loud

When children are learning to read, they are frequently encouraged to read aloud so that they can improve their reading skills. However, as we get older, many of us begin to practice reading aloud infrequently, unless we are asked to read something in class. But, it is a shame that more people don't read aloud when they are studying, as it is a valuable tool to improve learning and increase memory retention.

The fact is that reading aloud increases a person's cognitive ability to remember select information. This has been proven through a variety of clinical studies on the subject, which found that reading information aloud makes it easier to remember than reading silently. But, this is not to say that simply listening to information through an audiobook is a replacement for reading it out loud yourself. The study tested multiple types of reading materials, including reading silently, listening to audiobooks, listening to an audio of yourself reading, or reading aloud. It was found that reading aloud at the moment was the most effective option. The reason for this is because reading out loud is more successful because it requires more active involvement, giving it more impact in our memories. When you listen to an audiobook, it takes away this active involvement.

Although, it was found that if you record information in your own voice, you can remember it better than if it were in someone else's voice. This means that it can be helpful to record verbal notes on your phone or computer. By doing this, you can gain the benefit of reading the source material aloud to better remember it, but you can also listen to it later on if you need to remind yourself of any important information.

Use Ink and Pen (or Pencil) Instead of a Computer

There are many reasons to be thankful for modern-day technological advances. We can take notes more easily than ever, whether on a smartphone, tablet, laptop, or desktop. These allow us to take neat and easy-to-read notes more quickly and with less carpal tunnel than writing by hand. It is especially helpful for disabled people who have difficulty holding a pen for long periods. But, does that mean computers should completely replace handwritten studying notes by the general population? Not necessarily.

Studies have been conducted on the matter; these studies have not only examined writing by hand for taking notes during studying, but also in the classroom, giving us a full picture. These studies found that for memory and learning purposes, handwritten notes are superior.

More precisely, these studies found that handwritten notes both improve memory recall and the recall of vocabulary.

In another study, it was found that when students take handwritten notes in lectures, they are more likely to perform better in tests. This study actually found out that one of the biggest problems of taking notes digitally is that people are more likely to write them down verbatim. But, if you remember, learning and neuroplasticity are improved when you have to translate information into your own words. Because of this, when people have to save time as handwritten notes are slower, they are more likely to write the notes in their own words or as a summary of the topic. This increases cognitive function and actives the neurological pathways, allowing us to build deeper memories and better recall.

Lastly, it improves memory by requiring more senses and activating the area of the brain that improves comprehension and learning, as opposed to digital note-taking. This means you will not only better remember the information, but you will better understand it, as well.

Some other benefits of handwriting are that it has been shown to lower stress; improve creativity; increase deep thinking; writing about feelings can improve mood and promote general well-being; and, studies have found that writing about what you are grateful for before bed can improve sleep and general well-being, which will improve work both in and out of the classroom.

Of course, this does not mean that handwritten notes are the best for every circumstance. This is especially true for disabled people who may struggle with the task. While some professors have shamed their disabled students who require laptops for note-taking, this is discriminatory and should never be allowed.

Distribute Studying

It's important not to focus on studying for long extended periods or cramming, as you are less likely to absorb the information at a deep level. You may pass an exam, but you won't retain the information for much longer. This means that it is important to distribute your study sessions over a period of time, rather than doing it all at once. This may mean doing your homework over the course of summer, rather than doing it all right before back-to-school, or, it may mean studying a given subject a little every day rather than for several hours during one day of the week.

Distributing your studying and learning doesn't only apply to study sessions, it also means that you should remember to take breaks. But, many people will focus so much on trying to accomplish something that they forget to take breaks, which only backfires on their desire to progress.

Studies have shown that by taking regular breaks, you can reduce stress and increase productivity in the process. In fact, while you may be taking a break, your brain is still working on learning. A study conducted at USC and MIT found that when a person is taking a study break, the key regions in their brain for learning are still highly active. This study revealed that breaks are an important part of learning because while you may be resting, your brain is still working to actively consolidate the information you are taking in. It plays a key role in learning comprehension and multidimensional thinking. While you may have the urge to skip breaks if you are tight on time to study, remember, you won't learn as well if you skip them. Even a five or fifteen-minute break to close your eyes can help.

Test Yourself Frequently

By testing yourself frequently, you can greatly boost learning. Studies show a few reasons for this. First, similar to reading aloud, it allows you to take a more active role in the information you are learning as well as using more of the five senses. But, there is even more to it than just that. You also get to activate memory recall each time you test yourself, solidifying the neurological pathways. Lastly, you have the opportunity to answer correctly or incorrectly. Studies have found that when you answer incorrectly and then learn the correct answer, it creates stronger neurological pathways, allowing you to better remember it. This means if you mess up in your practice tests, you are less likely to mess up in an official test.

This can help you do better in school and make a good impression on your boss or clients. For instance, you might try testing yourself on any statistics, cash flow projections, sale estimates, or any other bits of information that are important. If you have to give a speech or presentation, then test yourself on everything you might say, including how you will introduce yourself.

There are many ways you can test yourself, but a few of the most common options are flashcards, online tests, questions placed at the end of each chapter of a textbook, or you could ask someone to lend you a hand in a pop quiz. As you are studying information, you might try writing down important information on two pieces of paper. On one piece, write a question regarding the information you want to remember. On the other piece, write the answer. You can staple these two pieces together for ease of use. These two sheets will allow you to quiz yourself (ideally speaking aloud) as many times as you would like.

Switch Up Your Approach

Often times, when people are trying to learn something, they repeat the same process time and again. For instance, they may continue reading over the same list of facts, hoping to memorize them. But, by continuously using the same study approach, you are, in fact, hindering your cognitive ability to learn the information on a deeper level.

Studies completed at Johns Hopkins found that if you actively switch up your study methods, even only slightly, you can better master a subject or task. Not only will you master it better, but you will master it more quickly. For instance, if you want to get better at drawing, you shouldn't always practice drawing the same subject. You should switch things up so that you can get a better grasp of the subject. Another example is if you are attempting to pass a biology test. Instead of always using the same study method of reading aloud the information you are trying to learn, switch things up occasionally so that you are using a variety of methods. This helps you to better remember the information and create stronger neurological pathways through neuroplasticity.

Let's look at an example of how you can do this:

1. First, practice rehearing basic skills or information. You should run through the information, presentation, or given the subject a few times until doing so feels natural, and you have a good comprehension of it. You will find that each time you do this, it gets a little easier.

2. Give yourself a break of at least six hours, which usually means waiting until the next day. Remember, as we previously discussed, your cognition will continue to process the information during your break, so this is an important step that shouldn't be skipped. This step allows the information to root more deeply in your cognitive pathways.

3. Practice again, but this time switch it up a little. Try speeding up your practice. This means you may read the information out loud at a faster pace than you usually would, you run through slides more quickly, or you quiz yourself with less time to answer the questions. You may make more mistakes, but that is okay, as these mistakes will help you better ingrain the

correct answer. Next, try the same process, but at a slower rate than you would usually go. It may seem easier, but you will find that even giving yourself more time will mix up the process enough to help you learn better.

4.   Try switching up your tools or situation. This may mean switching from the computer to writing by hand, changing from practicing at home to in a library, switching from quizzing yourself to having someone give you pop quizzes, or changing from reading aloud to listening to recordings of yourself reading the information. There are countless ways you can switch up your studying, and by doing so frequently, you will create stronger neurological pathways.

5.   Whenever you are learning something, it includes steps. This is true whether you are learning information in textbooks or actively practicing a new skill. Try breaking up your subject of study into smaller steps or chunks, then practice these individually rather than all at once. Wait to move onto the next step after you have mastered the current one. After you have mastered each of the steps individually, try putting them all back together again.

Improving Multidimensional Thinking in Kids

As discussed in this book, multidimensional thinking is an important skill to improve learning. But, some people, especially children, can struggle with this skill. While many people learn how to improve their multidimensional thinking to a point as they age, it can be overwhelming for a parent or teacher to help their child with this so that they can improve in school. Thankfully, these steps are known to help kids and adults alike.

Practice Bending the Rules:

Kids are often taught to abide strictly to the rules their parents, teacher, and society set. This is a good thing when the rules are good! But, overly rigid thinkers that struggle with multidimensional thinking will love and hold tightly to these rules, even fixating to the point of reminding the other kids around them what the rules are. The problem with this is that it holds them back from developing multidimensional thinking skills. The good news is that you can help a child practice bending the rules without actually breaking any important rules set in place. How? Games are a great teaching method!

Have your child pick one of their favorite board games to play, and then try changing some of the rules. The child may not like this at first, as they have a rigid mindset, but coax them into it. Soon enough, your child should learn that by changing the rules, you can make games even more fun. They will then learn to think on a more multidimensional level as they have to solve new problems and learn that rules are not always set in stone.

Teach Positive Self-Talk:

Learning to use positive self-talk, and actually using it regularly, is an effective way to work through problems and manage emotions. I emphasize the importance of this self-talk is positive, as it is all too easy to fall into the negative. When we are stuck with a problem, we often tell ourselves that "it's impossible," "I can't do this," or "I'm stupid." You need to avoid all this negativity with your self-talk. Instead, use compassion toward yourself while calmly and analytically discussing the problem with yourself out loud. While vocalizing it may seem like an unimportant step, as you have learned throughout this book by reading aloud and taking tests aloud, you can make more of an impact on your cognitive function than doing it silently. The same is true in this case.

Start by taking a few deep breaths to calm both the mind and body. Now, state what the problem is and examine several solutions. Try to come up with at least three solutions or more. Once you have examined your possible solutions, choose which one seems the best fit.

By practicing self-talk in this way, a person is able to learn to better cope with unexpected changes and react less with frustration when overwhelmed. This is an important skill for children and adults alike, but if you begin teaching it to children as they grow, it will already be a habit when they are older.

Switch Up Your Routine:

Routines can help a child feel stable, as they always know what should happen next. This can especially help working parents to keep order in life. But, having children on an overly strict schedule can produce rigid thinking. The child will no longer know how to cope with change or spontaneity, and it can cause harm to their mental health as they grow up and realize that not everything can be scheduled or controlled.

This doesn't mean you can't have a routine in place, but you should also practice spontaneity. For instance, if you always eat at home, maybe one night you can surprise your child by going out for dinner instead. It doesn't have to be expensive; it can be something as simple as McDonald's or Jason's Deli. Or, vice versa, if you usually eat out, try eating at home and letting your child help with the meal preparation.

Some other changes you might try are changing what time your child takes a bath; spontaneously watching a movie or reading a book together, randomly going to the park one evening; or, make an extra special memory by preparing breakfast for dinner and eating your meal as a family on the floor in the middle of a fort you and your child built together out of sheets and cushions.

The options in how you switch up your child's routine are endless. But, it is incredibly important as it will teach your child spontaneity, how to cope with change, and that it's okay to be creative and do things in a new or different way.

Fun Reading Material:

The Amelia Bedelia children's books are a great resource. You can get countless books in the series online and in bookstores at a low price. If you aren't familiar with the charter, Amelia is an overly literal maid that lakes multidimensional thinking. Because of this, she frequently makes mistakes and goes on fun adventures. By reading these books, you open up the opportunity to discuss them with your child. You can talk about how she made mistakes, laugh about it together, and talk about what she could have done instead with a more flexible and multidimensional approach. Of course, this is a more analytical look at it, but you can discuss it in a fun and lighthearted way with children that will still get the message across.

Similarly, you might try purchasing some children's joke books. Rigid thinkers frequently struggle to understand jokes and puns, but by using joke books, they can better understand how they work and become more flexible and multidimensional in their thinking. It is especially helpful if you, as an adult, go over the joke book with the child and discuss how different jokes work, word meanings, and what makes the jokes funny.

Joke books may not seem that important, but the multidimensional thinking they promote is able to help children learn better problem solving, increase their focus ability, and learn how to better engage with their peers. This skill won't develop overnight, but with consistent work and practice, you will see progress. This progress will not only help your child in the present, but it will continue to help them as they grow into adulthood.

CHAPTER 8: USING THE KEYS TO UNLIMITED LEARNING IN THE CLASSROOM AND GROUPS

There are many classrooms across the country, and the world, that look the same. In these classrooms, children are told to sit still and in uniform while they pay attention and do as they are told. This lasts for several hours before children get a short break and then must resume studying for several more hours. This rigorous schedule can be difficult for any student and doesn't promote multidimensional thinking or cognitive abilities. But, it is even worse for disabled students and those with learning disabilities or other differences. For these students, a school can become a torturous place where they don't fit in, and nobody is able or willing to help them learn in the way that their individual needs require. Because of this, many students are sent to "special" classes with other struggling kids, or they are forced to be pulled out of school all-together and homeschooled.

Many students are chastised for being unable to fit in and do as they are told. They appear to look like every other child, so why shouldn't they be able to do what other children do? But, the truth is every child's brain works differently. They all have different cognitive abilities, skills, and weaknesses. If this isn't taken into consideration, then the child can be ostracized, and a teacher may fail in their role to encourage the child through the learning process.

Simultaneously, there are many amazing teachers that want to help these children more than anything. They can see the struggle the child is going through and want to help them enjoy learning and develop their abilities. Yet, the teacher may not know how to do so. The child themselves doesn't know what they need, so the teacher can't simply ask. What should they do? Simply put, learning should be customized to the individual. By learning a variety of techniques, you can help each child out depending on their needs, so that they can each excel in their own way. In this chapter, we will be going over ways you can help such children in the learning process, so that any child, no matter their struggles, can learn and grow. Whether you are a teacher or a parent, you can teach children these methods to help them excel in the classroom setting. If you are a parent, discuss these methods with your child's teacher, so that they can be on board and help you help your child.

Start with Mindfulness

As we discussed in the previous chapter, mindfulness and breathing exercises can greatly benefit cognitive health, multidimensional thinking, and learning. But, while adults may use this tool, oftentimes, children are left in the dark without the knowledge to know how to complete the method on their own. One of the most powerful ways a teacher can prepare young minds for learning is to start class off with a minute of mindfulness.

Often times, when class starts, whether it is the beginning of the day or the start of an afternoon class, there is excitement and disruption. The transition between getting to school and starting class or the transition between classes can be a challenging one for all parties involved. But, by taking a single minute, only sixty seconds, you can help both the students and the teacher regain focus, calm their nervous system and breathing, and prepare the cognition for taking in new information and learning.

When you start the class, try dimming the lights and speaking in a calm voice. You want to make the atmosphere soothing and calming as possible. If you have young students that are seated on the floor, have them sit criss-cross applesauce; but, if your students are seated at a desk, ask them to sit upright with their feet planted flat on the floor. Student's hands should be rested gently in their lap, and their eyes should be closed if they are comfortable doing so.

Walk the students through the process. Tell them to imagine there is a string connecting their heads to their ceiling so that their head is naturally lifted, their spine is straight, and their chin is parallel to the ground. Have them focus on their breathing and the movement it causes throughout the body: the belly moving in and out, the shoulders going up and down, the airflow through their nostrils.

Now, have the students focus on how they are breathing. Have them take a deep breath in through the nose, hold it for a moment, then slowly let it out through the mouth. Have them repeat this process six to twelve times until the minute is up.

Remember, this shouldn't just be done at the start of the school day, but ideally at the start of every new class throughout the day. Try discussing the matter with the other teachers in the school, so that everyone is on board. By simply taking a minute to focus on breathing and relaxing, the children can let go of any stress that they are holding onto, quiet their minds, and focus on what they are at school for learning.

Promote Movement

When children are in kindergarten and preschool, teachers understand that they need to move around and give them the freedom to do so throughout the school day. But, as students get older, they are expected to sit and learn while being still. Because of this, students with ADHD, autism, and learning disabilities are chastised for being unable to sit still with the rest of the class. They are called a "distraction" and "disruption."

For students who struggle to pay attention to a teacher and sit still, it is better to find a way that you, as the teacher, can promote movement without causing a distraction for the other students. This is beneficial, as movement can promote memory, memory recall, cognitive functioning, motivation, and overall learning abilities. It is able to activate neuroplasticity and create stronger cognitive pathways, what teacher wouldn't want those benefits for their students?

Some teachers are doing this with fidget spinners. They set rules for the fidget spinner use so that it does not become a distraction, and as long as the students follow the rules, they can use the fidget spinners as-needed. These should only be allowed as long as they are a quiet variety of the toy, and the student isn't causing excess noise with them. If fidget spinners don't work in your classroom, then try the Tangle Jr. This is an alternative fidget toy that doesn't cause excessive noise or distractions. These can be purchased online.

Simple putty can be a great and quiet tool, as well. With this putty, such as the classic Silly Putty, a student can mold and work their putty in their hand without causing distracting noises or excessive movement. Plus, it is a cheap tool that is easy to come by! Even if a student has an allergy to Silly Putty, there are many different types of putty on the market they may use as an alternative.

Lastly, you may try bouncy leg bands, yoga balls, or wiggle seat cushions. Don't be discouraged if the first option you try doesn't work for your classroom. There are many options, and one of them is sure to help your students.

Sensory Break Time

Often times, sensory needs are only thought of for small children. But, older children and even adults may need sensory breaks. This is especially true of autistic students and those with sensory processing disorders. Remember, even if one of your students hasn't been diagnosed with one of these conditions, they may be struggling with undiagnosed symptoms. This means that you shouldn't discount a child's need for sensory breaks, simply because they have no diagnosed disorder.

If you find that incorporating a bit of movement into your student's school life doesn't resolve problems of restlessness, overwhelmed tension, stress, anxiety, fear, depression, or even aggressive tenancies, then your students may need you to go a step further in helping them. Often times, these students are showing external signs of an internal problem that is not being addressed properly. One key tool that often helps such students is sensory breaks.

You can schedule regular sensory breaks into the class schedule, or you can use them as needed for specific students. Let your students know that they can talk to you and ask for sensory breaks whenever they become overwhelmed. After all, an overwhelmed student can't learn. But, if they can calm down through sensory breaks, then they can succeed.

There are many different types of sensory tools you can use. Along with the fidget toys mentioned above, you can also try oral sensory bead necklaces, aerobics such as jumping jacks, deep pressure from compression vests and weighted lap pads, glitter bottles, soft blankets, water beads, sequin "mermaid" pillows or dolls, coloring books, Etch-A-Sketch, or noise deprivation with an eye mask and noise-canceling headphones.

There really are countless options, but what you use will depend on the child. It is best to have a variety of options; you can even have them written down on a decorative and framed list, and allow a student to choose whichever option that will best help them. While one child may need more sensory input by moving around or using a sequin pillow, another child may need to escape from sensory input with noise-canceling headphones.

Help teach students that when they feel the pent up stress rising, instead of getting frustrated, they should request a five-minute sensory break. You can have a timer for this purpose. With this break, they can calm down, reduce stress, and then come back to learning refreshed and able to process and take in the information.

Remember, this does not just apply to young students, but older students, as well. Seniors in high school may need these tools just as much as a young child in elementary school.

Strengthen Cognitive Skills

As you are well aware by now, if a person is an overly rigid thinker, they will struggle with multidimensional thinking and cognitive abilities. This can show itself in many ways, but it is especially commonly experienced in people that have learning-based disorders. Many children who are struggling and behind in school have underdeveloped cognitive abilities. To help strengthen these abilities, you can recommend a child's parents read this book and adopt some of the principles in the child's everyday life.

But, there are also online-based programs that can be used to help. One such program is Fast ForWord, which is based in neuroscience and specifically meant to help children struggling with reading and learning difficulties. The program comes designed for students starting in pre-kindergarten all the way to graduating high school.

This program is specifically designed to help children with learning by first improving their cognitive skills, such as processing speed, focusing ability, and memory. The program is individualized to each student's needs so that they get exactly the help they need. The program also teaches through reinforcing reading and language skills that the children need for school so that they can perform better in the classroom. By directly targeting a student's neuroplasticity and cognitive function, this program is able to help students improve from the ground up.

As Open-Ended Questions

Flexible thinking is vital to develop cognitive skills, creativity, and independence. One wonderful way to foster flexible or multidimensional thinking is to ask open-ended questions. These are questions that don't have a standard text-book answer. One answer is not necessarily right or wrong. Because of this, when teachers ask open-ended questions, it allows students to start exciting conversations, collaborate, explore new ideas, and even practice leadership skills. The creativity of these questions allows a student to examine the world and themselves in a new way, giving them a better glimpse of their own potential that they never before realized. These open-ended questions will not only help them in the classroom, but they will also help them engage in meaningful conversations with their peers out in the world. They will gain the ability to better analyze, understand, and communicate about real-world current events.

However, to avoid stepping on any landmine topics, be careful when asking questions about race, disability, minorities in general. This is not to say these topics should always be avoided, but teachers should be careful in how they deal with them, especially if they themselves are not part of that minority. For instance, there have been professors in colleges that have asked insensitive questions about the holocaust directly to their Jewish and disabled students. Open-ended questions are a wonderful tool, but a teacher should be wise in how they implement them, the topics they address, and the questions they use so that they do not potentially cause harm to their students and these minorities.

Work with the Student's Personalities

In this day and age, most people understand that there is a big difference between introverts and extroverts, though many people have a misconception as to what this is. Often times, people are viewed as extroverts if they can hold a conversation, even if they are true introverts. On the other hand, people may assume people are introverts because they are calmer and reserved when they are truly an extrovert. Then, what is the true difference between introverts and extroverts? Simply put, people are like batteries that need to recharge from time to time. An introvert is able to recharge when they are on their own, whereas an extrovert recharges by being around other people. While they may recharge in these instances, it isn't to say that they can't enjoy being around other people or enjoying alone time between sessions of recharging. If you truly want to understand your students better, ask them to take the Myers Briggs MBTI personality type test. These tests will not only tell you which students are introverted and which are extroverted but other facets of their personality, as well. Be sure that you keep a record of which personality type each student is so that you can research and understand their individual types, and then use this knowledge to personalize their learning experience.

When you are handing out class assignments, keep in mind that some extroverts might do better in group assignments, while some introverts might do better working either alone or in very small groups. Rather than just assuming what your students need, try asking them, so that you can ensure you are providing them with the best options. You may not always be able to fit the environment perfectly for every student, but you can optimize it to the best of your ability.

By making group sizes based on introvert and extrovert requirements, and student partner assignments based on personality and who gets along together well, you can ensure your students can learn better. After all, as you have learned, people don't learn as well, and their memory is impeded when they are stressed. But, if you are able to lessen their environmental stress, they can better succeed.

This isn't to say students never have to challenge themselves to work outside of their comfort zone. But, it is important to find a good balance between challenging one's comfort zone and prioritizing what situation one best learns in. By generally allowing students to work in an environment where they feel comfortable and confident in, you can then empower them better for the times they do have to work in situations they are less comfortable.

Use Risks and Failure as Tools for Learning

As you learned earlier in this book, mistakes allow us to better learn from the failure of the correct answer. This will allow us to make fewer mistakes on more important matters in the future. For instance, if a child fails to turn in their homework because they simply forgot and you give them a failing grade, then they are less likely to make the same mistake in college or in the workforce. This temporary minor failure sets them up for success in the future.

But, there is more to it to that. Studies show that cognitive function is improved when we make mistakes. This means that because of neuroplasticity, we are able to create stronger cognitive pathways that will help us learn the correct answers on a deeper level.

Lastly, failure as children and in school allows children to learn how to grow from failure. Rather than giving up and giving in, children can learn to use failure to motivate them to continue working hard and improve. This is a valuable trait that can only benefit them as they age.

You may want your students to succeed, but if you never allow them to fail, then they will be unable to learn from their mistakes. Of course, there are cases when allowances should be given, such as in the case of health, tragedy, or emergency, but in general day-to-day life, it is important for children to learn from their mistakes.

One way you may help your students with this is by giving them pop quizzes and practice tests, so that they can learn to fail and grow prior to taking official tests and exams.

Try a Flipped Classroom

The flipped classroom is becoming more popular, as teachers, parents, and students see the proof of its benefits. In this teaching method, students are assigned recorded lectures to watch and study as their homework. They then do their actual assignments, tests, and labs in the classroom. This doesn't create any more work for the student; it simply flips which work is done in the classroom and which is done at home.

Why try the flipped classroom? It allows for the most meaningful parts of learning, the activities, to be done face-to-face with direct teacher input. This allows the teacher to help students individually through anything they may be struggling with on a personal level. By doing this, a teacher can form a better relationship with students, help them excel in learning, and students will feel less stressed as they will be getting the help they need.

Instead of relying on relatives who are busy and overworked or ignorant on a given subject, the teacher can directly walk students through any confusion that is keeping them stuck on their assignments. Any gaps or misunderstandings are cleared up, rather than the child having to struggle with them week after week.

While the flipped classroom is quite a difference from many classrooms, it has been amazingly successful. According to the Flipped Learning

Network, 80% of students in a flipped classroom experienced attitude improvement, 71% of teachers saw improvement in student grades, and 99% of teachers reported that they would continue with a flipped classroom set up the following year.

The flipped classroom can help any student and teacher. But, it can especially help students who struggle with cognitive skills and learning disabilities. It can give every student, whether they have a disorder or not, a leg up to better succeed.

CONCLUSION

You likely came to read this book because you felt as if your current potential to learn was limited. Maybe you found this through studying at school and on your own, or maybe people even threw harsh words at you. Either way, through the course of this book, you have learned that this is not true. You have the potential to gain a limitless mind. You can attain the knowledge and learning you desire; all you have to do is put in the effort. Please, believe in yourself, as you can not truly lock into your potential unless you do. It may take time, you can slowly work on believing in yourself step-by-step, but in time, you can do it. You are capable of more; all you have to do is try.

Throughout this book, you learned how the brain uses neuroplasticity and cognitive function to further learning more than you ever thought possible. Whether you are tuning into this by reading aloud, studying in groups, embracing mistakes, changing your mindset, or developing your multidimensional thinking—you are sure to find learning becomes easier! Of course, to truly experience a limitless mind, you should practice all of the techniques in this book, and not only one or two. But, you can always work at slowly implementing them one at a time, to prevent from overburdening yourself. In time, you can adopt all the key methods for success, and it will be as natural as breathing.

Whether you are a student, parent, or teacher, you can succeed. You have all the tools you need.

Ingram Content Group UK Ltd.
Milton Keynes UK
UKHW020608250423
420723UK00006B/157